EARTH ENERGY
THE SPIRITUAL FRONTIER

Planet Earth is a spiritual frontier where we as spirit can create, learn and grow. Earth is the newest learning frontier for spirit and the most exciting. Here on Earth we have everything that is available throughout the universe.

EARTH ENERGY
THE SPIRITUAL FRONTIER

MARY ELLEN FLORA

CDM Publications   **Everett, WA**

You, the spirit, may develop and flourish in conjunction with the proper care of your body and mind. Therefore, the information in this publication is intended to assist you in your spiritual development and to enhance, but not be substituted for, any care you should receive from your licensed healthcare or mental health professional for the treatment of pain or any other symptom or condition.

Cover Art: Jeff Gibson

Art: Gail Coupal

Author Photo: Michelle Guilford, Yuen Lui Studio

Please direct requests to:

CDM Publications
2402 Summit Ave.
Everett, WA 98201

First printing 1996.

Publisher's Cataloging-in-Publication Data
Flora, Mary Ellen.
Earth energy : the spiritual frontier / Mary Ellen Flora.--1st ed.
p. cm.
Includes index.
ISBN 1-886983-03-8
1. Spiritual healing. 2. Meditation. 3. Earth -- Religious aspects.
4. Spiritual life. 5. New age movement. 6. Bioenergetics. 7.
Angels. I. Title.
248.4--dc20   1996

Library of Congress Catalog Number: 96-83587

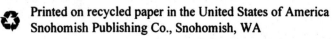 Printed on recycled paper in the United States of America
Snohomish Publishing Co., Snohomish, WA

Also by **Mary Ellen Flora**

The *Key Series* books and tapes

Meditation: Key to Spiritual Awakening
Healing: Key to Spiritual Balance
Clairvoyance: Key to Spiritual Perspective
Chakras: Key to Spiritual Opening

The *Energy Series* books

Cosmic Energy: The Creative Power
Earth Energy: The Spiritual Frontier

Books soon to be published

Male and Female Energy
Kundalini Energy

All titles available from
CDM Publications

ACKNOWLEDGEMENTS

Many people have helped with the production of this book. I wish to express special thanks to the main helpers.

Jeff Rice has been a valuable friend and advisor as publisher and cover designer.

Many thanks to Jeff Gibson for the beautiful cover picture and Gail Coupal for the fabulous drawings throughout the book.

Maggie Betteridge has helped greatly with editing, proofing, and encouragement.

Thanks to our proofreaders Reggie Taschereau, Lembi Kongas, and Stacy Smith.

Special thanks to my assistants Holly Gibson and Debra Rice for their support and validation throughout this project.

As always, love to my husband "Doc" Slusher for his encouragement and help.

With love and appreciation

this book is dedicated

to

Vivian and Paul Flora

my parents.

CONTENTS

Introduction...1
Earth Energy 4
Spiritual Rites of Passage on Earth.................19
    Conception..23
    Pregnancy 27
    Birth 31
    Birth to Three Years...................................36
    Four to Twelve Years.................................45
    Thirteen Years to the Present 54
    Death 60
Human Body Energy 65
The Astral Body:
Our Lighter Garment 96
Inner Space:
Spirit Creating Through Matter 103
Communicating on Earth..............................118
Earth Angels and Devils................................135
You and Your Larger Body:
Planet Earth..146
Earth Changes..156
Spiritual Techniques 163
    Grounding...168
    Centering in Your Head...............................171
    Creating and Destroying on Earth 174
    Earth and Cosmic Energy...........................177
    Your Aura..181
    Present Time 184
    Deprogramming...186
    Talking to God, Talking to Earth 190
NOTES...195
INDEX..197

*The Earth is your cathedral. Your body is your temple.
You are meant to be in harmony with all things.*

INTRODUCTION

The islands of Hawaii are a microcosm of our planet, with active volcanoes of flowing lava, majestic snow peaks, the restless ocean and peaceful beaches, verdant rain forests, deserts, plains and an endless variety of habitats. In these sparkling islands, earth energy is displayed with power and grace. Here Pele, goddess of fire, brilliantly represents the Earth angels just as the human residents represent peoples from around the world. The glories and variety of life in these islands can inspire all of us to grow closer to our planet and to learn more about the energies of the Earth.

I am fortunate to be in this wonderful place to write about the energies of the Earth. Every time of day and night brings new views of Earth and its power and beauty. Whether watching a peaceful sunrise or sunset or enjoying the power of a storm wind blowing the sea and trees, I learn something new about myself and the Earth. While watching the sun set over the sea, I am reminded of my childhood, when every evening in the summer I climbed a tree, watched the sun go down over the mountains, and wished it good night. As a child I thought of the Sun and Moon and Earth as my friends and talked to them as friends. When I got older, I forgot some of my childhood wisdom. Now I am remembering who I am and my relationship with our planet.

Everyone is meant to remember. Fortunately, there are those who never forgot. Some people are waking up slowly and some rapidly, while others still slumber in the heaviness of the material world. We are supposed to remember that we are spirit. We are meant to wake up to the reality that planet Earth is our larger body. We are to remember that our human bodies and our Earth body are our temples through which we are meant to create and communicate as spirit.

The upsurge in physical fitness, improved diet, and greater concern for physical health is no coincidence. We need to create healthy bodies to allow our spiritual energy to flow into the physical world. The concern with a healthier planet is also part of this waking up process. We are waking up and realizing that we have not been taking proper care of our bodies or our world. As we become aware of our spiritual nature, we also realize that we are supposed to treat all things of this world with reverence and care.

The Garden of Eden is planet Earth. We are the gardeners. Earth is such a rich, voluptuous, generous body that we lost ourselves in her. We stopped paying attention to what was healthy and balanced and put our attention on what gratified our senses. We developed the ego to cover the pain when we hurt ourselves in our misuse of our garden. It is time to wake up and remember who we are and that we are here to learn to use this body of energy to accomplish spiritual goals.

I hope that this information will help you wake up. You are spirit. Your body and the Earth are your creative space. You make a tremendous difference in everything you do, think, feel and create. Learn to love yourself, your body and your Earth and you will heal on a grand scale. If you have always wanted to heal the Earth, you can. Turn within and you will find the way to fulfill your very important part in the Earth play.

Together let us return our awareness to the wisdom of our childhood, when we all talked with the Earth and Sun and Moon.

EARTH ENERGY

Planet Earth is a spiritual frontier where we as spirit can create, learn and grow. Earth is the newest learning frontier for spirit and the most exciting. Here on Earth we have everything that is available throughout the universe. We have both ends of all dichotomies and everything in between. A dichotomy is a division of something to the point of opposition. We have a veritable cornucopia of learning opportunities in balancing these opposites to create union and flowing energy. While one may go to another reality to learn a single-sided lesson, one comes to Earth to learn how to make choices, learn balance, and grow to a new level of spiritual maturity. Earth provides a challenging spiritual opportunity.

A simple understanding of the game on planet Earth

and how we are meant to play it helps us recognize ourselves as spirit and the physical world as our spiritual creation. We are here to mature in our creative abilities, our power, and our energy. We have freedom in this planetary setting to choose whatever we wish. We are ideally meant to choose to return to God of our own free will. However, many souls have forgotten we are spirit and have chosen the material creations instead of the Source of creativity. This fosters fear and hate instead of love and creativity. A major challenge for spirit manifesting in a human body on planet Earth is maintaining a connection with God while creating in matter.

We can return to our original purpose of growing and learning as spirit by learning about how we are manifesting our energy on Earth and refocusing on our relationship with God. We are allowed to create beauty or ugliness, heaven or hell within this Earth to provide the widest spectrum of learning opportunities. We need to remember that we are learning and can use God's guidance to help us realize we are spirit and not the bodies or our other physical creations.

We as a human species are restricted to creating on our own planet, just as we as individuals are meant to create in our own body. Now that we are reaching beyond the Earth, we are being monitored, since we are not allowed to destroy our planet or the physical reality around us. As we learn about and gain power, we must remember to temper our power with love so that we create as spirit and not just as bodies.

Splitting atoms, focusing laser energy and harnessing many energies for power are all ways we are learning to manipulate energy. We are creating matter from our spiritual energy and learning how to manipulate it as we wish. Like children learning how to use our bodies, we make mistakes. Sometimes we remember that we are spirit and create accordingly. More often we forget and let the body we have created react to its surroundings instead of responding as spirit through the body.

Everything is energy. Some energy is invested in matter and some is not. The energy of planet Earth is energy manifesting in the form of matter. The energy manifesting in physical form moves much more slowly than the energy that is not creating form. For example, the energy of radio waves moves faster than the energy of the radio. You can see the radio with your physical eyes but not the radio waves.

Spirit is very fast-moving energy or energy of a high vibration. Spirit is creating through matter in the form of planet Earth. People can see a physical body with their eyes, but only those who use their spiritual sight can see spirit. Everyone and everything has a spiritual nature. Spiritual creativity in matter can be seen all around in human bodies, trees, flowers, clothing, food, and in everything that exists on Earth. All physical things are the manifestation of spiritual creativity. The Earth is an example of spirit creating in matter.

Earth energy is the cosmic vibrations that are invested in the matter of Earth. These vibrations are both seen and unseen. The faster the vibration, the more difficult it is to see it with the physical eyes. All physical matter that is seen is slow-moving energy. Earth energy is spiritual energy moving slowly to manifest as matter. Human bodies are the main investment of spiritual energy on Earth. The planet itself is also a manifestation of spirit creating in matter.

Everything on Earth is a spiritual creation. Everything is energy and all energy is in motion. We have forgotten a great deal of our spiritual information about creating with energy. An example of our creativity with energy that we have forgotten are energy lines, invisible to most, that flow around and through the Earth. Birds use these lines to migrate, and we can use these lines to control energy, move through space, and discover power centers such as Stonehenge. When asked by a teacher about how birds know where to migrate, an eight-year-old girl answered, "They follow the lines." Adults will eventually teach her the lines are her imagination, but energy lines are real and part of our earth energy resources. It is unfortunate that animals and children can use them, but most adults refuse to even be aware of their existence.

Earth energy lines are an example of physically unseen energy that can be used to create our reality. We use a great many other energies that we cannot see with our eyes. We use radio waves to communicate and microwaves to cook. We use laser vibrations to do surgery. Energy lines are there to be used, when we remember about them, as we have remembered about other energies such as microwaves. None of these energies, such as radio waves or laser vibrations, were invented; they were remembered or discovered like an old game put away in the closet waiting to be found. Earth energy can be used to create or destroy, to heal and to change things however we choose. We need to remember how to use energy consciously.

Energy lines also run through every physical body. Where many of these lines come together in the body, information and energy centers called "chakras" are formed. Where many energy lines intersect on the planet, we usually find a city, a ruin of past glory, or some other indicator of power such as Stonehenge, the pyramids or Mexico City. In our bodies we can learn to use the lines of energy to see the energetic motion which indicates health, balance, function and flow. Whether we view the lines of energy in our personal body or in the larger body of Earth, we can use these energy lines to work with the matter we are using. Like birds finding their way home, we can use energy lines to find our way through the physical world.

Unseen energy lines are only a part of the vibrations available to help us navigate our way through the physical system. The earth energy that we are most aware of is the energy we can see with our physical eyes. Everything around us is an aspect of earth energy. Bodies, human and otherwise, all of our physical creations, buildings, clothing and the million other things we have made, are all part of the energy invested in the Earth. Trees, flowers, dogs, cats, cars, houses, money, and everything we see and know of are part of spiritual creativity on Earth.

Earth energy, or the vibrations that make up the physical manifestations of Earth, moves more slowly than uninvested cosmic energy or the vibrations of the Cosmos not in matter. This phenomenon of slowing down energy to create is an opportunity for spirit to learn about creativity. Spirit, in its purest form, is not as focused as spirit creating through physical form. Sunlight shining through glass is focused and thus intensified. Spirit shining through matter is also focused and thus intensifies its attention on a particular creative cycle.

The development of spiritual maturity requires the completion of many cycles of growth. Part of the growth process for most spirit includes creating into and through matter. To us on Earth, this means creating a body and creating through that body. Fortunately, through reincarnation, we create many bodies to use in the process of learning about our spiritual creativity. By returning to Earth in a variety of bodies, we have the opportunity to learn an abundance of information. We can learn about the differences between male and female vibrations and how to use them. We can learn about the pull of the heavier, denser vibrations in matter and how to overcome them. We can learn about emotions and other energies of the physical body and how to effectively use them as spirit.

We learn a world of information while in physical bodies on planet Earth. We learn about time and space and how to manipulate them. We also learn about giving and receiving and balancing dichotomies, birth and death, how to communicate through the dense vibrations of matter, and about how to bring the energy of the body up high enough to be used by spirit. All of these lessons and many more must be learned before spirit can return to its Origin. Planet Earth and the energy here is a golden opportunity for learning many necessary spiritual lessons.

Earth is a planet of dichotomies. The creation of opposites gives us the opportunity to learn balance. We need to learn to balance all things. Healing is balance. When things are in balance, they work in harmony. If we are trying to be all good, we long to be bad. When we are being bad, we long to be good. By being in balance, we experience harmony and recognize that we have both of these energies within us and can control them. Every soul can experience either end of any dichotomy on planet Earth. That is the reason Earth is a challenging reality in which to learn and grow.

A soul may devote an entire life to experiencing goodness and another life to being bad in order to learn about both ends of this dichotomy. The important thing is to be in control of the learning experience and make conscious decisions. A young man I know was obsessed with being bad. He could not seem to stop himself from sexually molesting women or taking advantage of women whenever he could. He did a great deal of work in clearing the experiences of his present life to free himself of his obsession. Eventually he saw a past life when he had been a monk and had fantasized about women his entire adult life. He had not been able to live up to his vows of celibacy within his thoughts. He used past life fantasies to create his present life in order to balance his "good/bad" dichotomy; so he went from living what he considered to be "good" to living out his idea of "bad." He is still not taking responsibility for his thoughts or actions, so who knows what he will create in his next life.

As spirit creating through matter, we create with our thoughts, fantasies, deeds, words and actions. It is necessary to take control of all aspects of our creativity on Earth to create what we want as spirit. Any unconscious level of creativity can cause a drastic detour in the growth process. For example, if someone is harshly judgemental of something, he may return in his next life as the thing he judged. A soul who is prejudiced against a group may return as one of that group to learn their reality. What you resist you become.

This phenomenon of dichotomies is tied into what some people call karma. In this Earth reality what we put out comes back. What we create we have to deal with, if not in this life, in a future life. By balancing the dichotomies of Earth, we learn to create in harmony. In balance we find acceptance, neutrality, and spiritual control. We learn our lessons when we balance. We miss the lesson when we get out of balance on one end of a dichotomy or another. Ethics can interfere with the balance if we stop to judge ourselves. By allowing the full spectrum and free movement provided by dichotomies, we can take charge of our creativity by accepting ourselves where we are so we can move into balance. We can learn that all things are within us and we can balance within to take control of our creativity.

The purpose of dichotomies is to offer us freedom of choice. We can choose one end of the dichotomy or the other. We can choose anything in between the opposites, and we can choose to balance. Planet Earth is a place of dichotomies because we need the freedom to choose our reality for ourselves. We can freely choose God when we have the full spectrum from which to choose. We can choose physical reality or spiritual reality. We can choose light or dark, good or evil, God or man. We can choose to hate or to love. We are free to choose anything.

This freedom allows us to learn and grow. We learn what works and what does not work on both the physical and spiritual levels. We learn what the consequences are for different actions. Red Skelton played the part of a little boy who liked to get into trouble. He often said, "I'll get a whipping if I do this. I'll do it anyway." My husband likes this saying as he experienced this choice often in his life. He learned early that his choices were important.

We learn very young what actions bring us which reactions. We learn how to deal with the varying results. Sometimes we choose what benefits everyone; other times we choose what will make us feel better. We may choose what will harm another or ourselves because we want the gratification the action will supposedly bring. Our freedom of choice allows us to play the game of life. We play, we lose, we win, and we learn what works and what does not.

Do not be afraid of the game of life. We have many

lifetimes to learn to balance dichotomies and to create what we want as spirit. We can learn to take charge of our karma by taking spiritual control of our earthly creativity. We can learn to create what we need in any lifetime instead of trying to do what we believe we should, like the young man trying to be a monk when he was not in control of his sexuality. We can learn to do what is correct for us instead of pretending according to someone else's rules.

Balancing dichotomies is one of the main lessons on planet Earth. We learn to balance when we acknowledge that we are spirit and begin to consciously create in the physical world. Like my husband and Red Skelton's character, we must take responsibility for our actions, even if they will "get us into trouble." When we are consciously taking responsibility, we are in charge and the lessons are easily learned. Balancing dichotomies, so we can be in charge of creating our personal reality, is an important part of creating with earth energy. We take charge of the cause and effect aspects of karma. We know the effect of what we cause and take responsibility for it, and in doing so, we learn to balance.

Fortunately, on Earth there is time and space in which to learn our lessons and practice them. Time and space are both important gifts and lessons for souls in this physical world. Spirit outside a physical body is not bound by time and space. In a body, we have to learn to adjust to creating through time and space. This seems frustrating to spirit at first, but eventually we realize that time and space are a gift to allow us to rectify our mistakes and have the opportunity to try things as many times as we need.

Time and space are both spatial concepts. Time is a form of space. Matter allows us the luxury of space to experience our unique vibration. As spirit, we manifest into matter to make a space for our personal creativity. In this creative space we are able to learn about our vibration, our weaknesses and strengths, our lessons and goals. When we create a body, we create a place to express our unique spiritual qualities. We then make choices in relation to dichotomies and create our reality according to the choices. Time and space allow us to change our reality. If we do not like a choice, we can change it. Like the child doing something he may get in trouble for, we all have the time to change our actions and avoid the consequences. If we are driving a car too fast, we can slow down. If we are walking across the street too slowly, we can speed up. We can change our reality because we have time and space.

If there were no time and space, we would be bound by the mere idea of the action. Once we had thought of what we planned to do, it would be done. We would not have to create it through time and space if they did not exist. This level of creation, without time and space limits, demands spiritual maturity and responsibility. Our human species is working toward that but is not there yet. We still need time and space to make our mistakes and learn our lessons. We are still children and need time and space; that is why we have physical bodies with which to practice our spiritual creative power.

We are all like mischievous children and try many actions we know will create problems for us or others. We do have time to change our behavior. Time and space are our friends. They let us move slowly through the physical world instead of creating as rapidly as we can as spirit. We must slow down when we enter a body and use the time-space continuum to learn about creativity and about our unique effect on all other things.

For spirit without a body, or outside a body, there is no time or space. Spirit creates instantly, can be anywhere instantly, and can manifest at any time. When we have a body, we move through time and space. For example, we as spirit can instantly manifest from Oregon to Ontario, but if we have a body, we have to get into a car, drive to the airport, get into the plane and fly to Canada. Bodies offer challenges and opportunities to learn all kinds of things that we do not have to deal with outside a body.

Time and space are two main aspects in creating with earth energy. Patience is a way to manipulate time and space. We can learn to flow with the earth energy instead of fighting it. Patience is one way to do this. We are spirit and can experience our timelessness even while in a body when we acknowledge our spiritual nature. By realizing that all things will eventually balance, we can be patient instead of anxious about the outcome of any action. God is patient, as God is infinite and not bound by time-space limits.

Fortunately, we are limited by time and space while in a

body. This limit gives us structure within which to work and focus. We create and grow through time and space. A child creates, learns and grows in maturity through her life experiences through time and space. Time and space are like the easel of life on which we paint our personal picture.

The physical aspects of life, such as time and space, are presently losing some power. The experiences of life are speeding up as the vibration on Earth increases. When more cosmic energy flows into the physical reality, the energy of the physical world moves faster and comes closer to the spiritual vibration. This increase of cosmic energy is occurring on Earth now. The activity of volcanoes and earthquakes along the Pacific Rim and other areas of the planet as well as the weather changes are examples of this heightened vibration. Because the planet is like our larger body, it is also reacting to the increase in energy just as our bodies are reacting.

Life on Earth is a process of learning and growth for every soul here. We go through various stages of growth as spirit just as we do as a body. In the present the vibration of Earth is moving up so the species known as human can increase its vibration and continue to mature. We are meant to realize our spiritual nature and see that the body and the physical world are vessels for us to use in our creativity and growth. Children growing up experience vast physical and emotional changes just as we are experiencing as a species. We are a species growing up. Some souls are aware of this process, but the majority are still oblivious to the vast changes.

The Earth will waken many as she cleanses herself. This large body we have created is growing and changing to such an extent at this time in our development that we cannot ignore the entry of higher energies into our reality. We are all growing equally as fast as our planet. If we accept the spiritual nature of our growth and work with our physical creations, we can experience a great joy in this stage of life. If we fight our spiritual reality, we will be overwhelmed by the physical world and experience a great heaviness that will interfere with our experience of the light of spirit.

There are a thousand and one ways to work with the energies of Earth instead of against them. The simple act of blessing our food before we eat it clears the energy of the food and brings a blessing into us. Sitting quietly and listening to the sounds of the planet and letting them move through our consciousness, helps us know our Earth and harmonize with her. Looking at and admiring the beautiful creatures of Earth - robins, snails, bears, spiders, coyotes, whales, or horses allows us to learn about our own bodies and their place in the greater pattern. When we put our attention on Earth and her inhabitants, we learn and grow.

We can learn to view the world from behind our own eyes and see how to flow freely and easily through the vibrations here. We can learn how to communicate with the other creatures of this Earth and how to communicate with the Earth, with each other and with God. We are so much more than we are now aware, with talents and abilities beyond most people's understanding. As we open to these gifts, we become aware that caring for the Earth is a joyous task and one we are developed to do.

By working with the earth energies, we become the gardeners we are meant to be. By working as spirit, we regain our power and perspective. If we want to know when a volcano will erupt, we need to learn to ask the volcano and the diva or angel of God associated with that volcano. When we need something of the Earth, we need to ask for the abundance of the planet. We must learn to talk to our physical world again as we once did in the beginning of this physical creation. We can be as in touch with the planet as we are with our own body.

If you are not in touch with your body, that is where you need to begin to understand earth energy.

SPIRITUAL RITES OF PASSAGE ON EARTH

The spiritual nature of life on Earth is similar to the process of the body's development. Conception, birth, life and death all represent different aspects of spiritual development as well as physical development. Spirit creates through a body in order to focus its attention on a particular aspect of its evolvement. The body mirrors the soul's growth from conception or the spiritual idea implanted on Earth, to death or the return to pure spiritual form.

Every time a soul returns to physical form, it must relearn how to manipulate earthly energies. It appears simple outside a body, but becomes complex once inside a body, since spirit is simple and body is complex. The spirit must maintain its seniority over the body to retain its spiritual or simple perspective. Since the physical reality of matter is sensual, seductive, heavy and fun to play in, it is more of a challenge to retain seniority than most beings believe.

Every lifetime we choose a body according to what we need to learn. We select our parents because we need to learn something from them. For example, one may choose a mother who is strong-willed and a father who is weak-willed to learn to balance will. It is easy to get caught in the struggle instead of learning the lesson. People often become lost in judging their parents instead of looking at what they have to learn from them. By looking at interactions with parents, siblings and other family members as opportunities to learn a lesson, relationships take on new meaning.

The family is the main survival and educational environment on Earth, so this group is of great significance to a soul's development. In creating its life plan, a soul selects parents and siblings to offer the greatest lessons. While outside the body, it appears an easy task to balance one's will, but once in the body, the soul must gain and maintain seniority over the body. That same body is being influenced and programmed by both parents, the grandparents, any siblings and anyone else that comes in contact with the child. Without the heavy energy of the Earth and the body and everyone else's influence, lessons appear easy. Inside the body, the soul has a different view and experience. In the body, the influence of the physical world is intense and challenging.

There is guidance in selecting a life path. There are beings that focus on helping souls return to physical form. These beings help the returning soul look at the possibilities and choose the one most beneficial to his spiritual growth. The timing of the conception, the place to be born, and many other factors are planned to create the correct energy for the foundation of the life experience.

It is a great opportunity to create in a body on planet Earth. This environment offers total personal freedom. This freedom makes the opportunity a challenge as well. We have to take responsibility for our creations and actions while in a body. We have to take responsibility for the body. It is helpful to see what each stage of life offers us as spirit in order to take full advantage of the opportunity. Freedom is a blessing and a challenge as we make our choices through life.

Spirit goes through rites of passage within each life and from life to life. It is unfortunate that we stopped providing physical rites of passage in most modern societies. The formal ceremonies make the transition from one level of life to another more real and meaningful. Baptism, bar mitzvah, confirmation, weddings, and funerals are a few of the rites we still observe. These ceremonies bring meaning to life and allow the individual to be recognized as moving into a new stage of life.

During these main developmental periods and throughout life, we experience spiritual and physical growth. Our growth is of great importance in this world. It is part of the pattern of freedom that is necessary for us to balance the dichotomies of earthly reality. These periods of growth can be times of joy and times of confusion depending on the specific circumstances. If one is being valued as during a bar mitzvah, growth can be a time of joy. If one is grieving, as we often do at the time of losing a loved one, growth can be a time of disturbance. The significant aspect of growth is that it is an important element of our experience on Earth. The more we acknowledge the growth process, the greater meaning we create in our lives.

We need to be constantly changing and growing. Just as our bodies grow and change throughout life, we as spirit also need to continue to grow. If we believe that we have reached an ideal state and stop, we are guaranteed to eventually suffer from the cessation of motion. Fear, hate, doubt and other emotional states can also cause us to stop our own growth. The loss of motion causes further disturbance and we eventually create illness in the body. Motion is necessary for a healthy existence, and growth is part of the motion of spirit in a body. Many periods of growth are experienced both spiritually and physically, and while we cannot categorize all of them, we need to learn to accept and enjoy them as well as the main rites of passage in life. It helps to recognize that the body goes through stages of development and change to meet the need that spirit has to learn and grow.

Major spiritual stages can be broken down in various ways. The following is a simple method of relating to spiritual transitions in a body. The list is conception, pregnancy, birth, birth to three years, four to twelve years, thirteen years to present, and death. Each of these stages represents a spiritual learning process. By looking at your experiences during these periods, you can learn a great deal about yourself. You can learn to understand your growth process and how to be in charge of it. Meditating on each phase can bring insight and healing. You can discover patterns you created as a child that you no longer find useful. You can learn to know yourself with great depth and thus have more control over your creative process. Instead of creating from a childhood pattern, you can clear the pattern and create from a present time spiritual perspective. Meditating on what you have created through your life helps you to know yourself.

CONCEPTION

The physical conception is also the spiritual conception. It is the planting of the physical seed and the implanting of the idea of a particular soul into matter. Once the idea is in matter, the soul can create on Earth in a manner that it cannot if not in a body. Spirit is a diffuse energy and body is a dense energy. The density of matter allows the soul to create on Earth in a seemingly solid form. A soul can begin completing spiritual cycles and creating thought forms and other creative projects as soon as it is conceived.

One reason a soul will choose to be conceived and then miscarried or aborted is because it only needed to manifest in matter for a short time. A spiritual cycle can be completed and the soul can move on to another level of development. The parents also have their lessons in these circumstances. It is important to have a spiritual perspective when dealing with spiritual matters. If there is only a physical view of conception, birth and death, there would appear to be little meaning to life. It would also make one focus completely on the body and ignore the soul.

Present at conception are the soul being conceived, the mother and the father. There may also be angels, the spirit guides of the parents and child, the grandparents or any other souls interested in the arrival of this being. If the soul is important to a large group of souls, there will be a host of souls present for the event. The parents usually believe they are the only ones there because they are usually the only souls with bodies present.

The parents may be aware of communicating with the "baby being" during the event. Some people know that something special happened. Most people are only aware of themselves. One story helps show the spiritual communication that can take place. A young married couple was visiting friends on New Year's eve. After the party they retired to their room and made love. At the man's point of ejaculation, he heard a booming voice in his head say, "I am your replacement." The couple discussed the experience and the wife said she knew that she had conceived. The next morning they told their friends they were going to have a baby. Their friends were amazed and doubtful when they said it was due in nine months. The couple had a baby boy nine months later who definitely "replaced" his dad in his mom's affections.

Souls without a body do not have ethics as they do when in a body. The being wanting a body does not have the same consideration for the welfare of the parents that we in bodies would expect. The spiritual view can be quite different from the physical perspective. The soul seeks the optimum learning experience and works to create it. If the parents are in agreement, the situation can be a joy. If the parents or one of them are not in agreement, the situation can be unpleasant or confusing.

For example, a woman had six children by six different fathers. Each soul she conceived worked out an agreement with her alone and then chose the appropriate father to create the body. The father was then discarded as unnecessary as the mother and child had no further agreement with him. This woman was happy with her situation, in spite of its unconventional nature. She was fully aware of her spiritual agreements and happy to fulfill them.

A different story is a friend of mine who conceived a child on a first date as a teenager. She had the baby and with great difficulty gave her up for adoption. The child created the biological parents she wanted and also the parents she wanted to live with as she grew. This causes trauma for many people until they realize that there is purpose in the process. The purpose is creating the structure for the life lessons of the entering soul.

Another story exemplifying a soul's determination to

enter the physical world with particular parents and circumstances is a couple who knew that they were to have five children when they were first married. After having three children, they decided to stop having babies so the husband had a vasectomy. Another child was conceived and born anyway. The couple was determined to stop having children so the wife had a tubal ligation. Another child was conceived and born. There were no other children after the fifth one arrived. This example shows how powerful spiritual agreements can be.

The desire to enter the physical world at a specific time with particular specifications of body type, life situation, and so forth appear easy to a soul outside a body. The circumstances may be more difficult for the souls in the body. They may not be married or may be older than they wanted to be to have a child or some other extenuating circumstances. Ideally, the agreements among the three main participants are amicable for all concerned. The more spiritually in tune the parents are, the easier the agreements are to fulfill or end.

Conception is a very important event in any soul's earthly creativity. The higher the energy of the event, the more spiritual energy the soul can bring into the seed of himself. Look at your conception and you will learn a great deal about yourself. If you do not know the physical details, you can meditate on your conception and learn what energy you planted yourself with here on Earth. The energy can vary from harmony, love, and joy to rape, fear, and pain. The soul determines what it needs and then helps to create it.

You do not have to be caught in the energy of your conception if you are willing to meditate on it and clear any energy that limits you. You are spirit and are here to learn. Part of your time on Earth is to overcome the challenges you created when you selected your life plan. Your conception is your creation to plant yourself into physical matter. Know what that energy is, and you will know the energy you are creating through. You may have wanted to be conceived through two people because the body would be intelligent, large and of a particular racial type. You may have gotten all you wanted from these people once you were born. Meditate on the energy and you can heal it or own it, depending on what you created.

PREGNANCY

Pregnancy is the time the seed germinates physically and the idea of you grows spiritually. The importance of your selection of a mother is obvious when you realize that the two most significant energetic events in your existence on Earth are with her: your conception and your birth. During gestation, you are completely dependent on her for the life and well-being of your body. The baby experiences everything the mother experiences. The baby experiences the emotions of the mother, hears the same sounds, eats the same food, and experiences her life from inside the womb. Medical science is now realizing how much the fetus experiences.

Some friends of mine were driving through town with

their daughters, and the husband commented that they should eat at a restaurant they had passed. The youngest girl said she liked that restaurant, but her dad told her she had never been there. She corrected him with, "I went there when I was inside Mommie's tummy." The couple was amazed as they realized that the last time they had eaten at that restaurant, she was pregnant with this child. This same child told her preschool teacher what a wonderful mother she had and described what a good job her mother had done during her pregnancy and birth. She remembered details that amazed even her spiritually aware parents.

Pregnancy is ideally a time of protected growth. The body is created with bones, skin, internal organs, brain and all of the necessary parts. As the physical body develops, the spiritual body is also developing. The spiritual body is made up of the experiences, sounds, smells, emotions, and other stimuli that the soul stores in the form of mental image pictures. If the soul chooses disturbances during this time, it is important to meditate on the lesson that needs to be learned. The lesson may not be completed and could be affecting life as an adult in an adverse manner. Problems can be overcome even when the adverse energy is stored in the body at this formative stage. A spiritual perspective is a great help in seeing the issue clearly and seeing how to overcome it.

The soul in the fetal state stores information just as it does when in a complete body. Spiritually we store information in the form of pictures. We store within our body the impressions and experiences we have in the womb to be used during life. If mother is happy and physically healthy, we carry this experience of well being. If mother is physically ill, emotionally disturbed or in a survival situation, we have the experience of illness, disturbance and fear that we cannot explain in our adult circumstances. Many of the unexplained problems experienced in adulthood are problems created or collected while in the womb.

A friend had the experience of being beaten while in his fetal development. His father beat his mother while she was pregnant with him. He had difficulty letting go of the pain because the experience took place so early in his physical development. He believed that the pain was part of his body. It is easy to believe that whatever we experience at this fetal stage is part of the body as we are born with it. Experiences this deeply imbedded in our system can be overcome but require attention.

It is helpful to know the circumstances of your conception, fetal experience and birth. This knowledge allows you to know what you have stored within your system and what you are creating through in the present. Through meditation, you can find these mental image pictures and clear them from your physical system. You can heal many of the problems of the present by clearing past experiences, especially the ones during this period of beginning your physical form. The majority of your impressions of life are gained from conception to three years of age. It is important to get in touch with this time in your life. If you are having problems, you can determine if the issue stems from something that occurred during this formative period. Examples of the effect of the mother's physical experience on the fetus vary from listening to music and poetry to poisoning from alcohol and other drugs.

Babies in the womb are in touch with their surroundings from the beginning. This idea has only recently become popular. Fortunately, mothers have been aware of their effect on their babies for centuries. Most women take better care of their bodies during pregnancy than at any other time in life. They often introduce the baby to music, art and other things they want the child to appreciate. By realizing that she is influencing the soul as well as building a body, the mother gets a larger view of the enormity of the project of pregnancy.

We see the opposite of this view in the horrors of babies born to mothers who are addicted to drugs. These beings experience the reality of their mother in every way. They are born addicted, malformed, or physically hurt in some fashion. People can understand the physical circumstances and need to accept the spiritual aspects as well. Some of the beings who choose an addicted mother may have left a previous body as an addict and need to complete a cycle in relation to drugs. Other beings may have an agreement to help the addicted mother or may have judged a drug addict in a previous life. Whatever the reason for choosing such an entry into this reality, there are both physical and spiritual ramifications. The being needs both physical and spiritual care for it to manifest fully in that body. Without assistance, the soul will continue to create through the pictures and concepts it created and gathered in its fetal experience. Patterns of pain and disturbance can be carried from generation to generation through the concepts learned and relearned.

Ideally, the times of conception and pregnancy are intended to be spiritually focused. Most women describe a sense of inner peace even if they experience physical difficulties. The level of creativity within is sufficient unto itself. The spiritual significance of pregnancy is felt by most everyone. All but the most jaded of persons is moved by the vibration of a pregnant woman. The coming together of the spiritual and physical worlds can be seen clearly in this creative process. It is a physical statement of the spiritual manifestation in matter.

BIRTH

The birth process is the emergence into the world. The spirit manifests in matter as a separate, independent body. Just as the soul becomes a separate consciousness from God, the soul and body separate from the mother's body. Some consider this to be the most significant experience in the physical life. The energy around the birth is important to the soul and his way of creating during that particular lifetime. The experience of birth is intended to be a spiritual occurrence as well as a physical one. The midwives in the past were both physical and spiritual healers. They helped the physical birthing as well as the spiritual one. There is always spiritual help at a birth in the form of angels. They appear around the mother several weeks prior to the birth to help the mother and the entering soul with the transition. The acknowledgment of these spiritual helpers enhances the birth experience for everyone involved, including the mother, child and the physical helpers.

The soul is born into the physical world in its own separate body. Whatever is happening at that time becomes an impression the soul will keep throughout life, unless it learns how to clear past experiences through meditation or some other healing process.

Whatever is occurring on the planet or in relation to planetary influences is also part of the soul's life lessons. For example, all of us born during a time of war have lessons to learn about conflict whether we were involved in the act of war or not. Many souls are born during war to learn to develop peace.

If the birth is at a high vibration with little pain, the soul has a clearer view of life. If the experience is difficult with a great deal of pain, fear, or other disturbance, the soul must work through these impressions to create its life. The more the mother and the soul are in agreement about the birth, the greater the opportunity for a spiritual experience that benefits both souls. It is important for mothers to acknowledge their children as spirit and begin this communication as soon as they are aware of the conception. This spiritual communication creates a wonderful field for growth and creativity.

An example of this communication in action is a friend who came to me just prior to her birthing to get a reading and healing about the "baby being" and the birth. She wanted an easy birth and had talked to the baby being about what they would create together. The mother and child were in clear communication but the mother could not believe the information from the being because it did not agree with her intellectual information. This was her fourth child and she believed the labor would take a certain minimum time, but the being had told her the birth would take three hours and would be easy. I was privileged to watch the communication as the mother and unborn child communicated and the child reassured the mother about the birth. The child and I also reminded the mother of the spiritual beings that are always present at births to help the spiritual transition necessary when entering a body. The easy birth took place soon after that and took exactly three hours from start to finish. This soul that joined us in physical form is a true delight and has everyone enthralled.

I know of a very different experience from looking at an adult long after his difficult birth. The man is considered dangerous because of his violent temper and his difficulty in understanding reality as most people see it. He spends most of his time isolated from people or in a remote commune. When he associates with others, their experience is usually fear. He had a very difficult birth. He was in intense pain for a long period of time during his birth and so was his mother. When looking at his energy clairvoyantly, I saw a dark red energy around the top of his head which permeated throughout his energetic system. He experiences life through this intense pain. People in pain are often violent, moody, or difficult to relate to in some way as the pain interferes with their faculties. This man is an example of a soul entering life through pain and living life in pain. His birth experience could be overcome if he were willing to face his creation, but he has become addicted to his pain.

Besides the significance of the physical circumstances and energy of the birth, the soul's life structure is determined by the birth time. The astrological chart indicates the outline that the being has established for the lifetime and the chart is determined by the place, time and date of birth. This indicates how the soul will relate to other physical forms during a lifetime. By manifesting into matter, a soul affects everything in the Cosmos, and everything in the Cosmos affects the individual soul. The astrological chart gives some indication of this impact and interaction.

In some societies, priests were consulted about the best time for conception so a soul would be born in the appropriate time for its life work. This foundation does not limit the soul unless the soul allows the limits. The structure is something the soul chooses to build its life within. It is like choosing what instrument to play in the symphony this time around, or choosing the foundation for the house one will build. We have a variety of lessons to learn and the different relationships with the physical reality offer us the opportunities we need to complete our cycles.

Every decision is made by the soul. Agreements are made with the appropriate other souls to play the necessary parts such as the mother, father, siblings and other family members. A soul may make agreements with the doctor or midwife to deliver it in order to create the energy it wants at this important time. Misunderstandings can occur and other souls can interfere. However, the soul manifesting the body ideally has the lion's share of decision-making power in the creative process. The mother needs to maintain control of her body throughout the experience in order to create a safe space for both bodies involved. If a decision goes against the beliefs of the mother, she naturally prevails as it is her body that is the host. Negotiations can take place in the spiritual agreement-making process. The important thing is being conscious of the communication.

Even with open communication, surprises can occur. A soul may convince the parents that the body being created is a male body when it is actually female or vice versa. I know two couples who were convinced the babies they were having were boys until they were born girls. Both souls loved playing tricks and both dads wanted boys. There was a time of adjustment since everyone had begun to relate to the soul as a boy. The soul communicates in its own way and we need to learn how to interpret its messages. We also need to remember that spirit has a great deal of amusement.

A mother and child in spiritual communication during the process of the spirit manifesting itself into the physical world is a powerful creative team. The two souls can decide what they need and want to create and then manifest their creation together. This is done on an unconscious level for most people. Everyone needs to acknowledge the spiritual nature of life and begin to have this communication from conception through birth. Ideally, the spiritual communication will continue throughout life if the souls do not allow the body considerations to prevail.

Communication with the being that has been conceived, nurtured, and is being born is of the utmost importance. The soul is communicating with the mother and usually the father as well as significant others. It is up to souls already in bodies to remember that we are spirit and to talk to those still in completely spiritual form. This communication makes the process for the manifesting soul a creative and joyous experience. It can make the experience exceptionally meaningful to the others involved also. Spirit loves communication.

BIRTH TO THREE YEARS

Birth and the joyous energy around the welcoming of a soul into the physical world is the way we begin our time on Earth. As a newborn baby till the age of three, we are learning how to work our body and how to function in the physical world once again. Watch a newborn and you will see constant motion. The baby is learning how to move, grasp, eat, and do all of the physical functions she needs in order to relate through a body. This is a tremendous learning process. From birth to three years of age is the time of greatest discovery for the spirit as well as the body.

The discovery of a finger or a foot is extremely exciting. It is no surprise that we are so drawn to

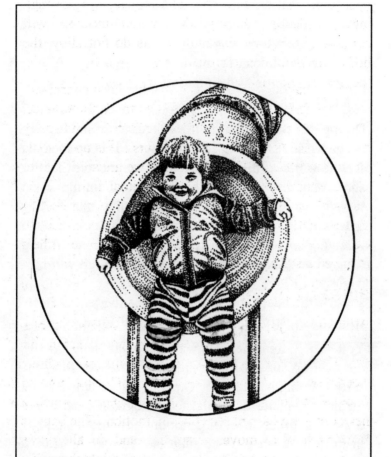

The soul communicates in its own way and we need to learn how to interpret its messages. We also need to remember that spirit has a great deal of amusement.

infants and small children since they have the joy of discovery that we all crave. Every second provides a new adventure. The baby is self absorbed in his world of learning to know his body. He gains mastery over his body and learns to move it on his own. He then begins the exciting adventure of discovering the world around him.

During this period of growth, we create our impressions of the world. If we experience love and acceptance, we see the world as a loving place. If we receive pleasure and instant gratification, we expect that from the world. If we have pain and deprivation, we believe the world is cruel and painful. As a baby and infant we are in a receiving space. We create our view of the world from what we receive. If a baby is loved, the adult will have concepts of love through which to create. If a baby is abused, the adult will have abusive experiences stored within his system through which he will create.

You can often heal unwanted adult behavior by discovering and clearing painful experiences from this early learning period. The experiences are stored in the memory as pictures, similar to photographs, and can be destroyed or drained of emotional energy that holds them in the system. The adult is a composite of these pictures from childhood, this life and past lives. You can alter your behavior by changing the composition of your pictures. Since the growth between birth and age three is extremely important in the formation of a life view, it is helpful to meditate on this period of learning to cleanse unwanted experiences.

We store these early impressions in our body and spiritual system to use in our next step of relating actively to the world. These new experiences are stored along with whatever concepts we brought with us into this lifetime. We may have a cycle to complete from a previous life and bring this into the present life. The new and the old concepts conflict and cause confusion. This confusion will last a lifetime unless one takes time to heal the internal conflict.

A young woman had a problem of confusing present and past lives. When I first met her, she was masculine in her looks and behavior. She was unhappy and confused most of the time. She had so much difficulty relating to physical reality that she could not work or maintain relationships with others. She was focused on a past life where she was in a male body. Most of her attention was on this past life when she had been a Buddhist monk. She had experienced abuse when she was a child in this life and was using some of her focus on the past as escape from the painful present. The conflict of concepts between the two lives was almost devastating. She brought ideals of peace and love gained through sacrifice from the past life while she experienced her present life as painful and unloving regardless of her sacrifice. She was so out of touch with physical reality when I met her that I wondered if she would ever gain her clarity. Fortunately, she was strong enough to commit herself to healing this conflict. She is now an attractive, capable woman who is married and working to help others heal.

As spirit, we are a universe of information and

experience. We bring a small part of that information into the physical reality when we create a body and manifest through it. We also gain more information through our conception, birth and life experience. Birth to age three is the most significant period of learning for the present life. All of this information is what we create with and through for the entire life. We have access to the knowledge and wisdom of the Cosmos as well. We have to avoid trying to intellectually understand this wealth of information so we do not feel overwhelmed by it. We can deal with one cycle, one event, one picture, one thought at a time and make great progress. We do not have to be aware of everything at once. By keeping a spiritual perspective and a physical awareness, we can be in balance and in charge of our creations. When we are overwhelmed by our creations by trying to do and know everything at once, we lose our enthusiasm and interfere with our relationship with God.

Keeping our spiritual work simple helps us progress easily like a one-year-old discovering himself. Thus, meditating on each cycle for a period of time and clearing that cycle can make healing easier. We can meditate on our conception, birth and life from birth to three years one cycle at a time, and gain insight into our spiritual purpose and clear barriers to our present creativity. If we remember that every soul is creating his or her reality, we can learn to respect everyone's creativity even if we do not agree with it. When we see traits and patterns developed from an experience at age two, we have a broader view of the situation.

Unexplained fears and disturbances often stem from something that happened before age three and is not consciously remembered.

This is the time that the being and the body realize they are separate from mother. This separation can cause trauma that is experienced in patterns through life. If the mother does not accept this natural separation of the child from her, she may invade the spiritual as well as the physical space of the child. The child may not want to be responsible for her own body and may cling to the mother to have someone be responsible for her.

The time period from birth to three can also be one of adventure and fun for mother and child as they discover each other as separate, unique souls each with its own body. It is definitely a time of adjustment as the relationship between mother and child changes rapidly and the child discovers its new body.

The relationship with father is also one of drastic and rapid change as the father suddenly has another body to deal with. The father often becomes angry in the first phase as he is often ignored and gains greater responsibilities. He can also experience a new joy as he experiences the physical interaction with the new soul in the family.

From birth to age three, the soul and everyone in its family experiences dramatic change. Everyone is called on to care for the body and everyone is busy making energetic adjustments to the new spiritual interaction.

When a capable soul enters this reality with the decision to work through difficult issues, it is easy to forget the enthusiasm with which the task was undertaken as spirit, especially if there is conflict between mother and father. A friend who has tremendous spiritual capabilities and a deep kindness encountered such difficulty on his journey. He encountered pain and struggle from his conception onward. His father beat his mother during her pregnancy with him. His father beat him and his mother until he was eighteen. At that time he woke up to the reality that he did not have to receive this punishment. He knocked his father down and told his father that if he ever touched him again, he would kill him. He left home and never related to his father again. He continued to help his mother.

He was a hard-drinking, tough-living man when I met him about fifteen years ago. He studied meditation, healing and clairvoyance and developed his spiritual abilities. His new spiritual awareness helped him regain his relationship with God. He continued to maintain an outward focus in his healing instead of healing himself. Countless times he was told that the problems he encountered related to the pain in the relationship with his father and his protection of his mother. From his birth to age three, his attention was on protecting himself and his mother from his father. He continued to focus on others with his healing energy because of this learned pattern.

My friend was in constant internal conflict between his spiritual beliefs and his physical experience. He had so much pain in his body that he eventually created physical illness. He also harbored a great deal of hate for his father that he did not come to terms with until the end of his life. In spite of his pain and difficulties, he remained steadfast to his mother and his friends. He was always available to someone in need. He did not give his pain and hate to others, like so many people in pain do, but sickened his own body with it.

Not until the end of his life did he allow himself to receive from others. In his desperate loneliness after his mother's death, he let his friends give to him in small ways. His agreement with his mother and their protection and nurturing of each other was so strong that he believed he had no reason to live without her. This dependence on his mother was created and developed during the pregnancy and first three years of his life. In some ways, he never moved beyond this early protective agreement.

My friend made the choice to sacrifice himself for others. This choice was at the beginning of his life as his agreement with his mother was to help her gain her freedom from abuse. He then created through the experiences of pain from his early childhood. He could not believe that he was loved by anyone except his mother until the end of his life. This lack of self worth interfered with his self healing but not with the healing work he did with others. This early agreement and the ensuing childhood experiences kept him locked into pain. While he fulfilled his purpose in this life, he could have experienced the enthusiasm he so longed to have by giving some of his healing attention to himself. He taught many people about neutrality, compassion, acceptance and love. He learned that he is spirit and a part of God.

We all have agreements with other souls to help us in our learning process. Most of these agreements are made before we are conceived. We establish the life situation that we want to have for the lesson we need to learn. We also establish the best opportunity to teach what we have to offer others. We can either fulfill or destroy any of the agreements with other souls. We establish the basic life patterns for fulfilling these agreements between birth and age three.

You are meant to honor your agreement to be responsible for your body and your agreement with God. If you do not like the agreements you have with your body and God, you need to meditate on them and clear other souls' energy, lies and interference of any kind. The interference is what disturbs you as it keeps you from being aware of your true agreements. You will find a sense of fulfillment when you consciously relate to your agreements with your body and God without interference.

The agreements you make with other souls may be fulfilled at conception, birth, or in the first three years of life. Many agreements are continued when they have actually been completed. Once the agreement is fulfilled, the relationship can take on new dimensions. A soul may disrupt its life path in continuing to focus on an agreement after it is already complete.

You need to look at your spiritual agreements as well as early childhood experiences. In this way, you find your path and regain your energy to follow it. This process is part of why we manifest into bodies, as we learn how to overcome different situations and how to enjoy life. Just as the baby and toddler are learning to use the physical body, as spirit we are learning to use our body as a creative spiritual space.

FOUR TO TWELVE YEARS

Once the soul has figured out how to work its body, it is ready to learn more about the remainder of the world. From the ages of four to twelve, the soul learns how the world around him works. The interaction with peers increases and has greater influence. The child's world expands with preschool, kindergarten and school. Many children experience other activities outside the home, such as scouts, church activities, sports, music lessons and an endless list of creativity. Every experience provides new material from which to create. Parents learn to let go and children gain greater freedom to create their own reality. By this age, the child is no longer so dependent on his parents.

My husband was a dentist for over twenty years. He worked with small children as soon as the mother would bring them into his office so they could get used to the dentist and the dental equipment without fear. He tells how pre-school children would fall asleep in the chair when he worked on them. These same children, after starting school, would return to him in fear because peers had told them that the dentist hurt you. The peer group information was more important than the children's actual life experience.

Between the ages of four and twelve, the child practices what she has learned from her parents, siblings and significant others. If she learned that crying got her attention at home, she may try crying at school to get attention. If that does not work, she will either be frustrated or learn other behavior patterns to get what she wants. The crying pattern will always be available to try under new circumstances. My husband tells the story of his first day at school when he was five years old. He lay down in his seat to take his daily nap and was whipped on his bare feet by the teacher for lying down in class. He changed his learned behavior quickly. At home he had to nap; at school he had to sit up. He was learning the ways of the world beyond home. He still enjoys an afternoon nap.

Between ages four and twelve, our physical and spiritual development is created from beliefs that we brought into the body with us and the beliefs we have developed from conception. This is the spiritual time of experimentation. We have learned to work the body; now what can we do with it? Is it worth getting whipped to take a nap? We have to learn to make decisions. We also learn about personal responsibility at this time. If we are not held responsible for our actions, we learn that belief. If we are told to take responsibility for our actions, we learn to do so. Some souls have a sense of personal responsibility even though they were not taught that value.

This time of experimentation with what we believe and the body we have developed can be very exciting. Every action is clearly an opportunity to experiment with our new power. Will Mom get mad at me if I do this? Will I get attention if I do what Tommy did at school today? Can I run fast, climb the jungle gym, learn to read? Everyone wants to try lots of things with the body to learn what it will do. We want to test our beliefs and skills and discover what works and what does not work for us.

At this age, we have been taught some ethics by our parents and others, but still we do not have the ethical levels of an adult. We have fun doing things and experimenting with actions and reactions that an adult would not consider. We do not have the same sense of good and bad that many adults have learned. A friend of mine, who had a four-year-old girl, gave birth to a baby boy. The daughter was at first excited about the new arrival but soon realized that the baby took attention from her. Her mother caught her hitting the baby on the head, obviously trying to kill it. The mother talked to her daughter and made her promise not to kill or harm her baby brother. The child understood exactly what her mother was talking about and agreed. This child is fortunate to have a mother who understood that she was not bad because she wanted to eliminate her competition. Her mother educated her that you cannot kill other souls' bodies without repercussions. The mother did not program her with ethics she did not need. To the child, death was not bad, only a transition out of the physical reality, and she wanted her brother out of her reality. This child has grown to be a sophisticated six-year-old who now takes knocks from her two-year-old brother without too much complaint.

This is the period of time the soul learns what works and what does not. Some souls never leave this level of development to move into adulthood. They continue to play with everything like a child. There is a time to grow out of the experimental stage and move on to the adult creative level. We need to do this both as body and as spirit. Ideally, in this stage of physical and spiritual development, the soul learns how to relate to the world in a balanced fashion. Too often people are taught to be out of balance during this time of development. Children are taught a great deal about what is good and what is bad, and these concepts go with them through life causing a separation between spirit and body. We are seldom taught that we are spirit and that our information needs to flow from our spiritual source. The main lessons are focused on the body perspective.

Between the ages of four and twelve, we learn our relationship with the world around us. We venture away from mother and father, encounter new adventures, different people and discover there are more ways to look at the world than we learned in our home. We learn new ways of relating and operating, and of course experiment with these new techniques. Some of this can be confusing as we discover that behavior which is acceptable at school is not tolerated at home and vice versa. The world is a vast arena of experience and experimentation in which we can play and learn from those around us. We carry into adulthood the information we adopted from others during this time.

The emergence and power of gangs in the lives of young people is an example of the need for strong group orientation and education during this time of development. Between four and twelve, we have a need to be part of something larger than ourselves and our family. It is a time for reaching out, experimenting, and learning. The gangs offer this, and there are few other opportunities for many young people. Society has forgotten the importance of rites of passage and the power these rites give to any group that offers them.

During this time of development, it is essential that the soul begins to make separations from its parents in order to develop a unique personality and way of operating. Too often families program the child to stay spiritually and physically a child rather than encouraging him to learn and develop uniqueness. This is a time when the soul and the body both need encouragement and support as it is a challenge to leave the safety of the family unit to become independent. Instead, the soul often receives criticism and interference causing dependency. The soul's experiences and interactions during this time color how it continues to view life.

A man I know was sexually molested when he was five. His mother was aware of this event but kept it a secret because of the social stigma and her fear of the father who performed the abuse. This man had unexplained fears and personality problems. He also was abusive to women and attempted to seduce or coerce as many women into sexual acts as he possibly could, trying to prove his masculinity. His adult behavior was similar to the behavior of a five-year-old boy. He would not listen to direction, blamed his actions on others, clung to his mother while hating her, and behaved immaturely in most aspects of his life. His mother followed him around and was always involved in his life. Her protection during his adult life interfered with his attempts to mature. This man was caught on the events that occurred when he was five. He had the opportunity to see and clear this experience but allowed his mother to block his growth. He eventually gave up the attempt to heal himself.

One of my co-workers has an amazing ability to deal with physical reality. She is able to deal with most any situation on a business level without getting emotionally upset. Everyone goes to her with their business problems and comes away feeling better about their situations. She learned as a child that she could handle difficult situations. Her mother was in the hospital when she was young, and her father validated her ability to deal with the situation and to be his helper during the difficult time. She has carried this level of self assurance with her into her adult life.

Every soul brings certain strengths and weaknesses into each life to help with the particular life lesson. Between age four and age twelve, one experiments with these abilities and liabilities. If a soul is focused on healing and is taught to be responsible for others, it will confuse healing strengths with responsibility for others. This confusion can cause a great deal of frustration as the soul tries to solve other people's problems instead of being a healing presence. The soul may have strength of intelligence. During this time, the soul will discover how to use that gift either as a benefit or a detriment to self and others. Depending on the environment the soul has created, it may choose to focus its gift to help be a banker or a bank robber. Either way, the soul uses its intelligence.

Most people are influenced in how they will use their gifts by school teachers they admire, their parents, clergy or a variety of significant others. It is an important time for the soul to learn what it needs to do instead of what others want it to do. A soul can take on someone else's desires for it and spend a great deal of life following another's path instead of its own path. This time of experimentation for the learner often frightens adults who are responsible for the child's welfare. The adults need to clear what they have within themselves that blocks faith in the souls they have agreed to parent or teach. Creating a safe environment for growth is easier when adults develop their own neutrality and tolerance.

My mother was worried about me at this age. I did not act like most of my peers and she was concerned about my finding my way through life as she knew it. My mother believed that a woman is dependent on a man for survival. She taught me this in hopes that I would find a man to take care of me because she did not believe I could take care of myself. She also encouraged me to get an education so I could support myself just in case no man would be interested in me. It took me many years to clear this conflicting information. I believed that I needed a husband and I believed that I needed to work to support myself. I lived with these two concepts by having a husband and working to support myself. I did not validate my contributions to my survival until I cleared the beliefs that I was dependent on a man for survival. Life is a great deal more enjoyable when you are certain of your ability to survive regardless of the likes and dislikes of others.

The changes that take place in the body offer an additional challenge during this learning period. The soul experiences the impact of the sexual drive and the hormonal effect on the body around puberty. The body develops sexually from birth on, but during the time of puberty, sexuality comes into full play and the soul must learn how it wishes to deal with this powerful aspect of life. The family and society dictate a great deal of one's response. The soul also brings in past life information and experience which influence behavior. Sexuality is often viewed through ethics instead of being seen as a natural part of creativity and communication, so the soul has to determine whether it will create through the ethics or not. The learned behavior colors the adult's sexual pattern in this life.

This is a time of intense change and development where the soul is challenged by the body as well as by external influences. Everyone at this age is constantly making decisions which are influenced by external forces as well as the body pulls. This is a time when one learns strengths and weaknesses as she deals with life on planet Earth. Can she overcome her own body's desires to create what she wants as spirit? Can she overcome the demands of her family and society to fulfill her personal life path? These questions are strong at this

Between the ages of four and twelve we learn our relationship with the world around us.

time. Late in this time, around age twelve, spiritual fervor is high and there is often a great deal of misunderstanding with others as the body is becoming an adult. During puberty, the strengths and weaknesses brought into the body and developed during childhood are tested in every aspect of life. A sense of adult self is established and carried into adulthood.

THIRTEEN YEARS TO THE PRESENT

The next spiritual stage in life is from thirteen to the present. During this time, the soul puts into practice all that it has learned. If one learned hate, that is what one will create with through life unless the soul takes spiritual control and clears the hate. If the soul learned love, it will create with love, unless it creates something to block that vibration in the life. This time is the creative period of using what has been learned to manifest one's spiritual purpose on Earth. For some this means a long time of cleansing and for others it means instant action. Whether one needs to meditate and clear during most of the adult life or jump instantly into creative action, one can operate as spirit in every aspect of life.

During the adult period we take what we brought with us into this body, what we have learned so far, and what we accepted from others and put it together into a life pattern. This pattern is the springboard of our creative accomplishments. Every soul has life goals. The early experiences are meant to establish the blueprint for achieving the spiritual goals. The adult time is for fulfilling the goals and continuing to learn necessary lessons for growth.

A difficult childhood is an opportunity to strengthen one's relationship with God in order to learn a lesson or to carry through with a challenging life. A close friend of mine had a traumatic childhood and followed it with an early adult life reminiscent of a soap opera. She learned a great deal about healing herself during these difficult times and is now helping other women heal themselves. She has the life experience to assist women with a variety of challenges. My friend has created a loving marriage and a joyous life work. She is an inspiration to anyone who wants to use tough lessons for progress.

Meditating on your adult life can bring you insight into your spiritual nature, lessons, and accomplishments. If you have gotten off track with your spiritual goals, meditation can get you back on your path. By getting to know yourself, you learn what you are here to do and see where you missed a turn or validate that you are going in the right direction for you. Adulthood is an important time to be awake and aware.

The time from thirteen to present may appear to be a long time for those who are fifty, eighty, or a hundred. The soul does not make as much change after age twelve as it does during the beginning years, unless it puts conscious spiritual attention on spiritual creativity. This is where meditation plays a key role in spiritual development. If a soul decides to review conception, birth, early years, past lives, and external influences, it will continue to change and grow at the same rate of development as it did in the early stages of life.

This is what Jesus meant when he said, "Come as a little child." If we consciously create as spirit, we continue to grow and change as we did as children. We are not caught in the concepts of earlier experiences. When we create in the present with the enthusiasm we had as children, we make a healing experience out of our entire physical existence. Every day can be an exciting opportunity, just as it was in childhood, if we see it as a time of spiritual creativity.

There are wonderful examples for us to follow in order to continue our spiritual growth. Buddha sat in meditation, reviewed his entire life, and cleared his pictures and experiences. He reviewed his past lives and healed himself of unwanted and unneeded concepts and lies. Buddha cleared his pain, expectations, and the other worldly limits that interfered with his relationship with God. He released his agreements with everyone except God. Buddha did the spiritual work and attained enlightenment. I do not believe that he did this without some struggle, like all souls in bodies. Buddha did accomplish this task and showed all of us that it can be done. He is a shining example of what we can accomplish as spirit creating on Earth.

Jesus also accomplished spiritual enlightenment in a physical body. Jesus came into and created through a physical body even though he was an evolved being who did not have to return to this world. He chose to return to help humanity wake up and free itself. The symbol of the cross, often associated with Jesus, represents his love of humanity, not his suffering. He loved the world so much he returned to a body to show others the way back to God. The cross symbolizes the body, and in taking on a body Jesus showed his love. The symbol is not one of suffering but of giving and love.

Jesus, like Buddha, loved so much that he was willing to manifest into a body which has effort, pain, mass, operates through time and space, and has all manner of physical limits. He moved from a space of light, freedom, all-knowing, and power and returned to us in physical form. His birth was the sacrifice and his death was the way-showing. His entire play on Earth was a display of love and giving as he separated his consciousness from the Cosmic enough to come into matter and show us the way out. He was willing to endure the physical world with all of its disruption and pain to help us remember God.

Buddha, Jesus, and other teachers created through bodies and remained senior as spirit to the pulls of bodies. They taught that everyone can accomplish this level of spiritual awareness while in a body. We too can create in matter without being overcome by time, space, mass and all accompanying aspects such as effort, competition, pain, doubt and so forth. We can learn to move through our stages of growth with spiritual awareness and enthusiasm.

Every soul can clear the past and live fully in the present. Every soul can do what Buddha and Jesus did. The time of physical adulthood is the time to attain spiritual adulthood. We are meant to learn that we are spirit and are here to create. We eventually need to attain spiritual adulthood. This is done by recognizing that we are spirit and then by clearing the unnecessary baggage that we have created and collected. Then we are able to create as spirit and manifest our unique spiritual message and vibration.

There are many examples of souls who have overcome their physical limits to bring the light of spirit into the world. Gandhi is a world famous example of spiritual seniority. He continued his growth into his adult years. He grew throughout his life constantly expressing the lessons he learned. He influenced the world by being himself as spirit. His lifestyle changed as he grew and changed. As he saw more of what was truth for him, he expressed it in his life. Gandhi was willing to give up his body for his spiritual beliefs and purpose. He changed the world with his steadfast message of love.

Unfortunately, the majority of Earth's population do not believe in themselves. People allow the early experiences of life to fetter them to a worldly existence and do not rise to the heights that can be obtained. Whether the accomplishment is physical or spiritual, it is still spiritual creativity. The young man who is only five feet three inches tall who plays professional basketball is an example of someone overcoming limits and attaining goals. Every soul has the opportunity to create a great deal during the adult time of life. It may be necessary to take some of that time to clear limits obtained in childhood. If we remember that Buddha and Jesus took time for meditation and personal healing, it is easier to face our own healing projects.

Encouragement is all around us. There are hundreds of people who have come from a difficult childhood and attained great feats. The people who are in school at thirty and sixty, learning a new way to create, are encouragement to everyone. The ones who volunteer to help others during their retirement years continue to grow and challenge themselves. On the other hand, some people who had a pleasant early life experience relate to adult life as a slave to physical reality. The choices throughout life give us the opportunity to choose our spiritual path or stay immersed in the physical world. Every soul decides his creative path from moment to moment.

Florence Nightingale, who is considered the founder of modern nursing, overcame familial and societal rules to follow her path. She left genteel society to work with women of lower classes in a profession that women of her class did not do. Her patience, perseverance and strength helped create a new healing opportunity in our world.

She had to overcome her early life training to accomplish her spiritual goals. Her lesson was not one of overcoming difficulty from the past but of having the strength to leave comfort and luxury to face pain and adversity as a champion of others in need. She can act as an inspiration to anyone overcoming pulls of the body, whether pleasant or painful, to create as spirit in this physical world.

Martin Luther King, Jr. is another example of a soul who chose the spiritual path. He overcame prejudice, hatred, and jealousy to create a nonviolent freedom movement that changed the world. He proved to people that love can work. His message to love the person and hate the behavior has lived on to help others create their reality in a spiritual manner. He would surely agree that one person can make a difference. That difference can be heard around the world when the soul establishes its unique vibration and follows its spiritual path.

Adulthood can be as exciting a learning and growing time as childhood. We are not all going to have the same impact as Gandhi, Nightingale, and King since our lessons and goals are different and unique. We can have an impact in our own world which ripples out to everyone. We can clear the hate, fear, and jealousy from ourselves. We can let go of the limits we learned and continue to grow and develop. Adulthood can be a creative and exciting time.

If the soul has a long sojourn in the body, it has an opportunity to use the latter years for meditation and spiritualizing the body. The last part of life can be like childhood backwards. This is one reason older people and children need each other's company. In later life we relearn how to leave the body just as in early life we relearn how to enter and use the body. Meditation on your death or transition into the spiritual realm can free you from fear and help you make this natural transition a spiritual experience.

DEATH

Death is the next spiritual rite of passage. At the death

of the physical body, the soul returns to purely spiritual form. The body is taken off as one would remove a suit of used clothing. Death is the transition from the physical to the spiritual or spirit transforming matter back into energy. Most societies have a great deal of ritual surrounding death. These rites of passage, like all other rites, are usually for those left behind in bodies. The soul is free of the physical world and all of its trappings. Most death rites are to help those left behind deal with their emotions. A few societies offer assistance to the soul making the transition out of the body.

The soul leaving the body can do so easily and simply if it chooses. The soul can create pain or struggle in the transition also. The death experience is the creation of the soul. The soul decides how it will die before taking the body. The decision can be changed during the life. The soul may spiritually mature and realize that it can let go of the belief that suffering is necessary in leaving the body. It can then create an easy transition leaving the body. The death experience is part of the soul's agreement with the body.

Death ideally is a simple transition. It is easier than conception and birth as it does not need to involve any other souls. Death, or letting go of the body, is between the soul and its body. Family and friends often become involved with trying to keep the body alive against the needs and desires of the soul. A family came to me years ago seeking help with the impending death of the father. He had cancer and was in a great deal of pain. He wanted to die, but the family was holding on to his body. He believed that he was supposed to die three years earlier and was aware that his wife and sons were holding him here. He and his family received spiritual information and assistance in understanding his transition. He died three days after he and his family received the spiritual information. His family was able to release him, and he was free to go on to his next journey. One of his sons was so moved by his father's spiritual experience that he decided to study to help others in their spiritual transitions.

The soul is connected to the body by a silver cord. When it is time for the soul to leave that body, it simply disconnects or severs the silver cord. It is important to finish the lessons and agreements with that body cycle before leaving the body. If the cycles are not complete, the soul will have to repeat the cycles in another body until they are completed.

A spiritual perspective is essential in relating to death. If you view death from a physical perspective you will experience fear and confusion. The body does not want to die when it believes that it is all there is. When you, the spirit, educate your body and become senior to it, the fear is overcome. Death then becomes a natural part of life on Earth. By destroying one body you are able to move on to the next body and the next lesson. You can learn to take the awareness you gained during a lifetime with you to the next stage of development. Your present life consciousness can go with you, the spirit, when the body dies.

Since death is a transition, death is both a beginning

and an ending. You end one life cycle and you begin another cycle of growth and change. There are many books written recently on death and near-death experiences. The near-death experiences are souls who left the body and moved toward the spiritual realm but returned to the body because it was not their time to leave the Earth plane. They describe the transition from physical to spiritual reality. They talk of the helpers there to meet them, the sense of peace and love, and the awareness that they are not their body. Everyone describes a new view of life and greater spiritual awareness after returning to the body.

These experiences and their documentation are to help everyone awaken to the fact that we are spirit and we do not die. Only the body dies. What we know of as death is the transition of the soul out of the body and its return to the purely spiritual state outside matter. In these times of major Earth changes there will be a great deal of death, and everyone will need to gain his or her spiritual perspective to benefit from this time of transition. It is not something to fear but an aspect of our creativity we need to be in charge of and use. From a spiritual perspective it is as simple as moving from one house to another or changing our clothing.

Spirit grows and changes through each of these transitions. From the planting of the idea of self at conception to the withdrawal of energy from the material world at death, the soul is learning and in motion. Part of each step in the process is learning how to overcome external influences and the pull of the material world and the physical body. The soul has a constant challenge to maintain its unique vibration during the life. Every life is an opportunity to remember that we are spirit and our agreements are with our body and with God. The remainder of reality is often attempting to get us to believe otherwise, so we need our spiritual awareness to accomplish our goals.

We are born into this material world to learn and to contribute. Our manifestations affect everything and everyone. If we create love, everyone experiences it. If we create pain, everyone experiences that also. By manifesting what we spiritually came to do, we fulfill our agreement with the Cosmic Plan. The more we create and participate, the more we are able to learn. By letting go of fear and increasing our enthusiasm for life, we take up our creative challenge.

Manifesting in a body is a challenging spiritual opportunity. Every phase is a new creative opportunity. From conception to death, it is an exciting play, and you are the writer, actor, and director. As the body develops from immaturity to maturity, ideally so does the soul as it learns how to manifest and create in matter.

Birth is the opportunity to create in matter and death is the way to withdraw from matter. Birth and death appear the same to spirit: a new beginning.

HUMAN BODY ENERGY

The human body is an exceptionally sophisticated machine. It breathes, talks, walks, self cools and heats. It is self-lubricating and very efficient in fuel consumption and elimination. The human body is intellectually capable beyond our present comprehension and learns easily. It makes complex decisions and has quick responses. The senses are sharp and draw attention to the physical world through sight, sound, smell, taste and feel. The body is so capable that it is a challenge for spirit to control and focus it. The body wants to take over and create on its own. The soul has to gain and maintain seniority over the body at every stage of development. Spirit must learn how to operate the body and its functions, how to communicate with the body, how to relate to sexuality and emotionality, and how to maneuver through time and space.

All of these lessons are part of Basic Body Class 101 that every soul must complete. The advanced classes move on to levitation, telekinesis, astral body projection and other spiritual ways of using a body. The basic class is more than most souls accomplish as many do not gain seniority with their sexuality and emotionality much less learn to master time and space. Unfortunately, some souls try to move on to the advanced levels before they are ready and have to repeat the basic level. This can create spiritual imbalance and what is commonly called mental illness. There are many examples of capable souls who skipped some of their training and used their abilities in a manner that harmed them and others.

The soul also must maintain seniority over all the other souls that want to control that body, such as the parents, grandparents, siblings and other influential associates. This is a challenge as the soul is dependent on others for the body's survival from conception to the time it can take care of the physical body around the age of four. Others are constantly programming the body with their information and concepts about how to live and operate in a body. Some of this information may be helpful, but a great deal of it must be cleared in order for the soul to fully function in its own body.

The human body is such a vast universe in itself that I will limit this section to certain aspects of the body and its impact on spiritual creativity. The aspects are: the intellect, sexuality and emotions, major body parts and their relationship to spiritual creativity, and communication with the body.

Spirit and body both love to communicate. It is important for us to establish clear communication with our body to create through the body. Communication between spirit and body is focused in, but not limited to, four main areas: the crown chakra (energy center) at the top of the head, the sixth chakra in the center of the head, the fifth chakra at the cleft of the throat and the second chakra just below the navel. The seventh chakra contains our ability to know, the sixth chakra contains the ability to see spiritually, the fifth chakra contains communication information and the second chakra has information on sexuality and emotionality, which are aspects of the body's will. Spirit communicates through the inner voice in the fifth chakra and with pictures, symbols and vibrations through the fifth, sixth, and seventh chakras. Spirit connects to the body at the base of the seventh chakra. The body communicates to spirit through emotions and can learn to talk with spirit through the inner voice in the fifth chakra.[1]

You as spirit can teach your body to communicate with you, and you can learn to understand the emotional messages of the body. Establishing your communication with your body creates a powerful creative environment. You know what is happening with your creative vessel, the body. The body knows what you are doing with and through it. For example, if you decide to write a spiritual book and neglect to tell the body what you are doing, it will eventually rebel.

The growth necessary to bring the spiritual information through the body demands clear communication so the spiritual information does not get blocked by body or foreign energies. A dialogue allows the body to let spirit know when it needs a time out and gives spirit the cues about what healing needs to be done to continue the project. Spirit can enlighten the body about what it is doing through it and continue to raise the vibration of the body so the flow of energy is easier.

You can use the essence of this example in any situation. If you are considering getting married, you need to know the desires of both spirit and body. Communication allows you to make a decision that involves all aspects of your creativity. Without the dialogue you may marry someone you do not love spiritually or someone you do not desire physically. In marriage it is more pleasant if both spirit and body are served. Many marriages have been founded on the desires of two bodies and failed.

You spend a great deal of your time and energy on your work. Have you ever meditated on what work you as spirit need to do to best fulfill your purpose? Have you communicated with your body about what it likes to do? You may discover that you and your body can harmonize if you communicate. This communication will help you identify information that does not belong to you, so you can meditate on clearing the foreign energy and begin to create what you want. Your work needs to be your spiritual creation, not someone creating their desires through your body.

Communication with and from your body will teach you how much you have allowed your body to be programmed by others. Everyone has received and accepted programming. Toilet training is a form of body programming. Prejudice and hatred are other forms of programming. You can discover the unwanted programming in your body and learn to deprogram your body and spiritual system. This requires commitment to a spiritual perspective and continuing dialogue with your body. You need to realize that you have programmed yourself as well as others so you do not get lost in judging those who have programmed you. You may even find some programming you like and want to keep.

Habits or body patterns are part of this programming process. You or others have taught your body how to function and it operates from that pattern until you change it. You may have been taught to brush your teeth every night and your body automatically goes for the toothbrush before bedtime. You may also have been taught to be afraid of dogs and you cross the street whenever you see one. You may want to continue the toothbrush habit and change the habit of avoiding dogs. By becoming spiritually aware, you can discover the cause of the pattern and change it.

Talking with your body will uncover what is yours and what is not and what you want to keep and what you want to clear. Meditation will help you clear the foreign energy and information that you do not want to keep. This is a process that takes time as you have been accepting information from others since conception.

You can create a much clearer relationship with your body and God by removing from your body anything that is not yours or is not appropriate.

You are easily programmed through ethics. The concepts of right and wrong, good and bad, carry with them preferred states for which you need to strive. You are punished when you are "bad" and rewarded when you are "good." This form of programming starts when you are in the womb and continues through life. The rewards and punishments are strongest from birth to age three. After age three, you are able to move away from external rewards and punishments more easily and begin to create your own experience. By then you have internalized most of the ethics you were taught.

Most of the ethics we accept as the foundation of our world are rules created by our particular society to ensure a certain behavior. An anthropologist will validate that most ethics vary according to the society. There are only a few rules of human behavior that carry across most cultures, rules such as stated in the Ten Commandments of the Judeo-Christian heritage. Most of the rules tell us what not to do. The Ten Commandments have eight "do not's" and two "do's". Jesus lists the two "do's" as the important rules: "love God and love your neighbor as yourself." If these directions about what to do are followed, the other rules are not needed as we are already listening to God and respecting others. This connection with God would eliminate invasion such as murder, rape, theft and so forth. What would the world be like if everyone stopped and asked if their action was in agreement with these first two commandments?

Most people do not have an awareness of themselves as spirit, so loving God is not real to them and listening to God seems impossible. Instead of listening to God, most people look for the rules about what not to do so they will not get into trouble. I have been supervising people in their work for many years. I have observed that everyone wants rules to follow so they will not get in trouble. The individual who will operate from his spiritual awareness and make decisions without looking outside for information is unusual. The individual who looks to God for guidance is a rare gem.

Ethics are often used as a replacement for God and personal responsibility. With God one knows the correct path. With personal responsibility one can follow that path. Ethics can become rules to follow for those who do not wish to know themselves or God. The common belief is that if you follow the rules, you will be acceptable to God and to fellow humans. Too often the demands of the rules keep increasing, and one devotes a great deal of time to the rules and puts very little attention on God. This can become a process of intellectualizing God. What do I have to do to please God? This becomes an endless process of trying to figure out what God wants and always turns into humanizing God. Learning to listen to God is more effective as we do not need to memorize rules. Fortunately, God loves us exactly as we are.

Ethics are beneficial in that they keep some people in line with the ideal of loving God and neighbor by punishing them if they kill or rob. Laws and other forms of ethics defining what is good and bad, what is right and wrong, attempt to limit the actions of those who would invade and harm others. Ethics help those who are not in touch with God to limit actions based on fear and hate. People who do not need rules to act in a loving way find it difficult to accept many ethical rules blindly. Young people are especially upset by foolish regulations and ethics without meaning. The schools in the U.S. are in jeopardy because they no longer focus on personal responsibility, and the government has made it illegal to focus on God in public school. Instead of spiritual guidance or personal responsibility, the youth are given rules to follow that often have no bearing on living a spiritually focused life or even on living a personally responsible life.

Programming about what is right and wrong is part of what we have to clear from the body in order to fill the body with our unique vibration and creative information. There is a belief that people are evil and must be programmed to be good. In reality, we are spirit in a body, and the spirit must learn to be senior to the body and the false information stored within it. The ethics we are taught often get in the way of the communication between spirit and body. We have the safety of the first two commandments with which to measure all of our actions. Many of the other rules are group survival tactics and limits, including prejudices about what groups are good and bad.

When we operate as spirit and communicate with God and our body, we know the correct action in any situation. We do not need the programming about what to wear, what to eat, who to know, how much money to have, who to like, who to hate, what kind of education to have, who to marry, how to worship, what emotions to have or not to have, and an endless list of ways to act and function. Unnecessary rules create fear and fear is the opposite of love. By operating as spirit we create what we are here to do, finding the "do's" in life easy and light and the "do not's" easy to avoid. Love becomes a natural part of our creative process instead of a rule that cannot be followed.

Meditation can help to clear unwanted programming. You can learn what is yours and what is not, what you want to keep and what you want to let go of. The more you clear what is not yours or not appropriate for you, the more you create your way. This clarity enhances your communication with your body because you no longer have to talk through all of the noise of this foreign energy. A process of deprogramming is described in the spiritual techniques section of this book. You can use the techniques to increase your ability to talk to yourself. When you can talk with yourself, you can talk with God.

Your inner voice sounds just like you do when you talk. If you are hearing another voice it is not you. Meditate on clearing the interference and meditate on establishing your inner voice connection and you will soon hear yourself. You can use the spiritual techniques found in the Key Series[2] or those in this book to help you begin your inner dialogue. Communication between you and your body is necessary for you to create consciously in the physical world.

Your way of being in touch with Earth and its energy is through your body. You must learn to communicate with your body to create with and through it in harmony. Not talking with your body is like having a marriage where there is no communication, with each partner going his or her separate way. This can be very confusing when it is you and your body. If you go in one direction and your body goes in another, neither of you will fulfill your desires but will be at odds. This internal conflict will create confusion, disturbance, and interference with your purpose. The body is created to work with you. You need to talk with it and remember how it operates to use it effectively. When you as spirit are in control and communicating, you do not need so many external rules to help you create loving behavior.

Many souls who are spiritually focused forget to communicate with their bodies. This can cause frustration in creating what is wanted in the physical reality. If the soul is always slightly outside the body, and not consciously using it, the soul will create more on a spiritual level than a physical one. This is appropriate for some souls and their lessons, but most need to create through the body to fulfill their giving and receiving cycles on Earth. Some souls become so out of touch with their body that someone else has to care for the physical body in their absence.

The body has a need to feel real and it will use any means to do so. The body usually chooses food or sex

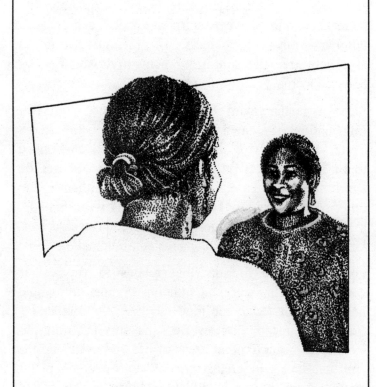

Your way of being in touch with Earth and its energy is through your body. You must learn to communicate with your body to create with and through it in harmony.

to make it feel alive but will use pain also. We can learn to make the body feel real by filling it with our spiritual energy and paying attention to it. Establishing communication between spirit and body can solve a number of physical problems. This communication can also help free the soul from being overwhelmed by body concerns.

Survival is the main concern of the body. Survival information is located in the first chakra, or energy center, near the base of the spine. Spirit is challenged to be senior to all of the ways the body focuses on surviving such as effort, competition, violence and other body energies. By communicating with its body, a soul can develop seniority over the survival drives. Understanding the body helps the communication.

One of the body traits that relates to survival is competition. In a survival situation, competition would help the individual get food, shelter, clothing and a mate. In our modern world, this survival trait has expanded to many other areas of life and even into the spiritual levels of creativity. When we compete for another's reality, we invalidate our own creativity and our unique relationship with God. We can see how survival traits have overwhelmed spiritual creativity in many areas. Pain is a survival energy that has been expanded to a belief that "one must experience pain to spiritually evolve". This is nonsense as pain is simply a signal to the body that its survival is threatened. Spirit needs to learn how the body functions and to be in charge of it instead of confusing survival issues with spiritual creativity.

The family is the main survival unit on Earth. The soul has to evaluate what it learned from its family and discard inappropriate survival data, such as "don't play with matches". Since the human body is a herd animal, gaining seniority over the herd instincts is a challenge. We often keep information that is not useful because it came from the survival group. You may have difficulty lighting a candle because of this old data. Mastery over the body's concerns is a major spiritual accomplishment and requires discipline and commitment.

Being spiritually in charge of the survival of the body may be a challenge but it can be very helpful in creating a safe and happy life. In a workshop I recently presented, one of the participants acknowledged this need to be spiritually in the body and connected with the Earth while doing physical things. She had been in several car accidents and realized during a meditation exercise in the workshop that the accidents happened because she was outside her body. She as spirit was not present to take care of the physical reality. She was delighted to find the solution to many of her problems was so simple. She simply needed to be in her body and grounded to the physical world while doing physical things.

The main way your body talks to you is through the emotions. Every emotion is a signal about what is happening in the body. When you are in touch with your emotions, you can learn to be in control of your body. Denying or ignoring emotions is not communicating with your body. You do not have to be overcome by the body's message either. You do have to pay attention and learn how to interpret the information to be in charge of what you are doing. For example, if your body is telling you that it is afraid, and you do not pay attention, it may behave strangely for the circumstances. If you pay attention to your body and see that it is in fear, you can respond. You may discover that the body is responding to you having your attention in the future. Since the body cannot be there, it is afraid. It could be reacting to a past experience that has been activated in the memory by the comment of a friend. If you as spirit focus in the present, you can bring your attention from the future and deactivate the emotions of the past experience.

You can be in charge if you know what is going on. You cannot be in charge if you do not pay attention to what you are creating and what is happening in your body. Your sexuality is another area through which the body speaks loud and clear, if you listen. Bodies have a desire to create, and one way they do that is through their sexuality. If your body is attracted to another body and communicates this to you, it is helpful to pay attention so you can be in charge. If you allow your ethics to block the communication with your body, it may act out the desire in other ways - eating, being angry, buying things and so forth. You can be in charge by simply acknowledging the attraction. You do not have to act on the body's desire.

You can move your emotional and sexual energies through your spiritual system in a neutral manner. You as spirit can learn to control your emotional and sexual energies for your spiritual purpose. This takes time and attention as you must talk with your body and get to know it. You have to slow down as spirit and pay attention to the experience of the body. When you do this, you learn about yourself as spirit since you are the one creating the reality. If you are allowing the body to be in control, this is an important lesson in itself.

You may have had the experience of feeling out of control of your anger. You can meditate on your anger and discover what you have created so you can take control of it. You may learn any number of things about how your body uses anger. Your body may be expressing anger with you for not paying attention to it or not taking care of it. It may be telling you that it is afraid and using the anger to attempt to move out of fear. It may be telling you that someone or something is invading it or that it is channeling someone else's anger. If you communicate with your body, you discover what the anger is about and can make the necessary adjustment in your energy or life to regain control of that emotion. This is true with any emotion.

You can also control your sexuality. Most of society teaches that others control your sexuality. Advertising, lessons in male-female roles, media and other sources teach that sexuality is stronger and more powerful than you and that it is more important than anything else in life. You can take control of your sexuality by communicating with your body about it. Get to know your body's sexual energy and how you want to relate to it and you will avoid a great deal of confusion. Many others want to manipulate your sexual energy to get you to spend money, perform favors, or fulfill their desires in some way. You need to know yourself to avoid being manipulated through this energy.

The ethical considerations around sex have stopped most people from getting to know themselves sexually. Many people allow others to maneuver them so they can say they were not responsible for their sexual actions. It is necessary to remove sexual ethics to have a clear communication with your own body about its sexuality. The ministers who preach about sex as a sin and then become involved in the sexual acts against which they preached are examples of souls who are not in control of their own energy. Ethics act as physical rules but do not stop the unwanted action when the body takes control. It is similar to a child doing what he is told not to do simply because the forbidden aspect of the act adds excitement. What we resist or judge in others, we end up creating for ourselves.

The more we know about something, the greater our control. Knowledge provides power. We are able to control the body when we know and understand it. We lose control of the body by ignoring it, giving up responsibility for it to someone else, or pretending that is does not have all of its aspects of emotionality and sexuality. I once overheard a woman say "I do not have any negative in me." She was referring to "bad" and saying that she is all "good." If this were true she would not have a body. We all have positive and negative, good and bad, and the emotions and sexual drive that we associate with those opposite poles. When we are in a body, we must learn about the body to control it and create what we desire through it.

The body is our vessel, and it has certain physical characteristics such as emotions, sexuality, appetites, senses, desires, limits, inherited weaknesses and strengths. We create the body to learn particular lessons through it. We learn our lessons easily when we accept the body as it is and communicate with it. We sabotage our creative goals when we ignore the body or pretend it does not have body traits. Everyone who has a body has emotions, sexuality, senses and desires. The level of seniority with the body and its traits is strongly affected by the amount of communication with and understanding of the body.

The intellect is an aspect of the body that we need to understand and use creatively as it is the upper level of the body. Spirit knows a great deal more than the intellect can comprehend. The intellect is similar to the computer that runs a machine, such as the computer system of an airplane. While the plane can run on auto pilot, it functions better when the pilot is in charge. The body can function without spirit in it or even paying attention to it. The body will act on its intellectual and emotional information rather than by direction from the spirit.

The intellect thinks, studies, analyzes, doubts, questions, and comprehends its environment to determine the best choices for physical creativity and survival. Spirit sees and knows what is best for the creative moment. When spirit works with the intellect of the body, creative outpouring is exciting and multifaceted. If one uses the intellect only, creativity is limited because it is held within the constraints of what the intellect can comprehend. The creative process is constantly questioned and doubted when the intellect is in charge as the process is limited to the physical perspective and there is no spiritual certainty.

Spiritual awakening is easier for those who are not enamored with the intellectual perspective of life. The intellect is meant to help us create more effectively in the body, but it has become a barrier for many in recognizing spirit. The intellect demands physical proof for everything, but there is no physical proof for many spiritual phenomena. Doubting and questioning are helpful in physical matters, but can be an interference in spiritual matters. Spirit requires faith, and faith is a step beyond the intellect. Spiritual faith is the main reason those not encased in an intellectual cocoon can experience spiritual phenomena more easily.

The intellect is meant to be used to improve spiritual creativity and learning on Earth, but many have become lost in the intellect and have difficulty moving above it. The intellect has become a god to some, and something to be feared by others. The intellect has often been used to create an incredible number of limits to spiritual creativity instead of being used to assist souls to create more effectively. The educational system is now caught in intellectual limits. Total intellectual focus limits growth to that one aspect of existence. While the intellect is important to develop, it is not the only level of capability or the best manner of discovering information.

Albert Einstein was said to have had trouble with math in school. This is probably because the presentation of the material was intellectual and not intuitive. Einstein worked on an intuitive as well as an intellectual level. His revelation that energy and matter are equivalent required his spiritual abilities as well as his physical intellect. In <u>On Science</u> he wrote, "Imagination is more important than knowledge." Many of the great scientists stated they have received inspiration for their work while asleep. This indicates that they received the information when they were outside of their body and not using their intellect. They brought the information from the spiritual level into the physical reality. These were souls who had developed the intellectual acumen to comprehend the information they had brought into their body. Often we need to move beyond the intellect to achieve the creativity of which we are capable.

You can use your body effectively by developing your intellect and remembering that it is not an upper limit, but a tool to be used to create through the body. You will lose your spiritual seniority with your body if you worship the intellect. This aspect of the body will become your god and will act as a barrier to your relationship with God. This can affect every aspect of your life, from health and wealth to inner peace. The intellect is best used with amusement, but instead we have developed it into a very serious game.

The health professions of today are an example of the intellect being used as a limit. The barber-surgeons of the Middle Ages were the beginning of the health professions of today. They did not include spiritual information or abilities in their healing work, but worked only with the body and physical perspective. This has continued into the present. Fortunately, the health professions are beginning to see that physical health is related to a great deal that the intellect cannot comprehend. There are many documented cases of miracle healings that cannot be intellectually explained. These healings happen because of the use of spiritual abilities and faith.

By combining spiritual abilities and the intellect, we can create a new level of sophistication in caring for and healing our bodies. The competition of the body with spirit causes many of the blocks to this potential union of skills. Many have gotten lost in an intellectual quagmire of competition, proof, doubt and other limits caused by being focused totally on an intellectual perspective. The reemergence of faith in relation to creativity is a step in the process of human maturation. Now that humans have discovered the benefits of the intellect, we are realizing that it is not enough by itself. The intellect needs to be combined with the spiritual energies of faith, clear sight, and knowing.

Scientific studies, the medical profession, general education, and other intellectually focused areas are beginning to mature into the realization that there is more to life on Earth than the body and the intellect. The intellectual arena is new in the course of history and immature in some parts of its development, especially in the belief that the intellect is the ultimate. The spiritual perspective brings the awareness that the intellect is one more tool that we have to help us create on this planet. We are like children who have just discovered sex. We believe it is the best thing in the world but do not know what to do with it yet. Games we play with atomic energy are a good example of our immaturity and our need for caution as we grow up intellectually.

We can watch an earthquake and realize that there is no way we can intellectually explain or affect the movement of the Earth. Our attempt to intellectualize the right way to construct an earthquake-safe building or predict through intellectual means the next earthquake shows clearly that the intellect has severe limits. Our spiritual information, communication, and abilities are what we need to use in this time of high energy and dramatic change. Many things are beyond our intellectual abilities and comprehension. We can use our intellect effectively when we realize that we are spirit and the intellect is a physical skill we can master and use to create on Earth. We need to operate as spirit to meet the needs of our present experience. Physical systems such as telephones can break down, while spiritual systems, such as telepathy, will continue to work regardless of the physical situation.

Every aspect of the body is for us to use to create our reality. The brain is one aspect of our creativity, and other parts of the body give us creative powers as well. Body parts lend themselves to spiritual creativity just as different stages of physical development mirror spiritual evolvement. Each part of the physical body is an aspect of spiritual creativity. The head is the spiritual control tower containing sight, intellect, knowingness, memory and control of all body functions. The brain contains the memory or stored information of the spirit. The physical eyes are in the head and so is the spiritual eye, thus the head contains our inner and outer sight. Spiritual knowing as well as physical knowing are located in the head. The head is our throne room in the temple of our body.

You can learn about your spiritual creativity by getting in touch with your body or any part of your body. If your eyes are not seeing well, you can meditate on what you do not want to see or what someone else does not want you to see. You can learn how you are creating as spirit through your body by paying attention to your body. If any part is unhealthy, you can learn what you are not doing correctly and then correct the physical or spiritual imbalance. Every part of your body represents aspects of your spiritual abilities and your creativity on Earth.

The bones of the body represent structure both physically and spiritually. Problems with the bones of your body indicate problems with the structure of your life. You can learn what you are creating by putting your attention on your life structure. You may be attempting to structure your life the way your father did his. This could cause problems in your life and in your body because you cannot fit into someone else's frame. You may have created hatred for your father if you believed he was forcing you into his structure and this could get stored in your bones. Cancer can develop if the hate is not removed and the structure changed.

As a child I injured my right arm in a fall, breaking the cap of the elbow. Years later I see this as an attempt to be like my mother and sister. They used their male and female energies in a different way than I used mine and I was attempting to balance my energy like theirs. That required shutting down my male vibration and the use of my male energy in my creativity. I fell on my right side which I associated with my male vibration and broke the arm, which represents creativity on a physical level. The broken bone was meant to restructure my energy to use more female energy and less male energy. The injury put me out of balance and made my body afraid because it was not operating the way it was meant to operate. I am still working on overcoming this error in judgement that I made through competition with another's way of operating.

Bone structure is formed in the womb and in early life. This developmental time sets a certain structure for life just as the astrological chart sets a structure. The structure can be changed and healed. Work on this level requires concentration and focus as the bone structure is dense. The denser the matter in which the spiritual energy is imbedded, the more focus is required to affect it. Altering the bone structure of your body takes your spiritual attention and power just as restructuring your life style takes discipline.

The spine is a major carrier of energy through the body. It holds the body erect, carries the nervous system, and blood vessels. The spine is the main channel for kundalini energy which is a very important energy the soul uses to heal and spiritualize the body. Cosmic energy channels run along the spine and the chakras are located along the spine. The spine is as important to the spiritual system as it is to the physical system. It is the "back bone" of the entire system.

Problems with the spine are often inexplicable in physical terms. They can be spiritual problems such as energy not flowing smoothly through the spine or the chakras. Spinal problems can also be caused by foreign energy in the spine that blocks the flow of energy. Learning to move spiritual energy through and along the spine can help with healing and proper use of the spine and enhance the well-being of the entire body.

Every part of the body can be related to spiritual creativity. The intestines relate to our creativity. Both male and female bodies create from this area of the system. Female bodies have the extra creative level of the female organs. The intestines and anus are often undervalued in their creative impact on the soul. Many societies teach only that they are unclean or are something of which we do not speak. As spirit, we need to own every part of the body and use each part as it is meant to be used. A spiritual perspective helps one see the purpose of the body for spiritual creativity.

The intestines are a creative center, and when owned and used spiritually, they offer a force of creative energy that is missing if this area of the body is ignored or abused for being "bad." Often people store emotional energy in the intestinal area such as hate, fear, or bitterness. This can develop into a physical illness if not cleared. The old saying about "swallowing" something you do not like is literally true for some. I knew a physician who died of stomach cancer because he could not "swallow and digest" the pain and agony he encountered in his work.

The creative energy of the intestines can be used in all of life. We can learn to create with this power by meditating on it and clearing any energy we have stored there that interferes with our personal flow of energy. Obvious foreign energy is that of the mother who taught us how to eat and how to eliminate. Emotional vibrations can also block the creative flow. We need to release pain or anything that gets in the way of our free flowing creativity. The interference will eventually develop into a physical problem.

You learn a great deal about yourself and learn to love your body by acknowledging that every part of your body is an aspect of your spiritual creative system. This is the reason you plan what type of body you work through in a life so you will have the characteristics and physical make up you need. You will have the challenges and advantages required for you to accomplish your goals. Talking with your body and different parts of your body will help you work with it. Tell your body you appreciate how it looks and functions, and you will create a better relationship. If a part of your body is not functioning correctly, talk to that part and you will put your spiritual attention there for healing.

You do not have to study anatomy to understand how to use your body, although it may help you. You can meditate on any aspect of your body to learn its purpose and meaning for you. Your body will bring your attention to any part of it in need by illness or injury if necessary. You as spirit can take charge and put your attention on the areas that need your attention before your body gets hurt seeking your attention. Your body is an amazing creation that needs your energy and attention. You as spirit can create your purpose through your body by owning and healing it. You can experience the joy and enthusiasm of physical and spiritual creativity when you acknowledge that your body is part of your creative universe.

Every cell in your body is a world in itself. Your body was created from a single cell. You are spirit and in charge of all of the cells in your body. When you consider how many cells there are in your body you realize what a large universe you control. You can see what a force you have to work with as you validate that every organ and physical system in your body is for your creative use. Each one has purpose and meaning for you. You become the master of your universe by getting to know and own it. Your body is your creative communication system on planet Earth. Know your body and you know the Earth. Know yourself as spirit and you know God.

The glands of the body are information centers that run your body and your creative system. You can learn about your personal system by getting to know your chakras and the glands associated with them. The adrenal glands are associated with your distribution of energy. For example, will you use your energy to fight or flee? You can learn about your creativity by looking at where you are expending your energy. Are you creating what you want or what someone else wants? Are you fulfilling your personal goals? Are you letting yourself have all the energy your body can handle or do you hold back? If you have indigestion or other chronic stomach problems, you may not be using your energy distribution correctly. You can have a great deal of fun using your energy to its fullest extent.

The gonads relate to how you create your reality in this physical world. Your body's gender of male or female is a significant aspect of your creativity. You automatically emphasize certain physical characteristics by choosing one gender or the other. These two types of body have distinct differences. Your creativity will manifest quite differently in one or the other. The gonads have your gender information; and the first chakra, associated with the gonads, has your information about how you will relate to the world. Unfortunately, some people have been trying to convince everyone that gender does not make a difference when it does. The choice of your gender affects every aspect of your creativity. The gonads are therefore an important aspect of your spiritual creativity. They represent for you as spirit your way of creating your survival and basic physical needs and how you will deal with physical creativity. The information is stored here about how you want to work, eat, clothe yourself, and generally relate to the physical world. This basic survival information is a cornerstone for your entire creative process.

The heart is associated with affinity or your relationship with all other things. The heart relates to the fourth chakra, which acts as a control for the other creative centers and helps you control your use of power and your emotions. If your emotions are not in control, your heart will pay part of the price. Your fourth chakra keeps you in touch and in control. Ideally, the heart is more for your internal creative system and less for your external interaction, but you may be using it more for your relations with others than for your relationship with yourself. You must first have affinity for yourself before you can have it for anyone else. You control your environment by controlling yourself.

The heart has more attention than many of the other body parts because we have put so much attention on it. The songs, poems, stories, movies, plays, cards and so forth about the heart or matters of the heart go on forever. We sometimes expect more of the heart than it can give and do not use the other organs for their jobs. We can use the heart most effectively by using it to bring internal affinity and control. As it pumps the blood or life force through the body, it creates affinity among the body parts and makes them whole. As it brings this life force, it can help control our use of power and our communication of emotions. The affinity aspect of the heart creates wholeness. Without affinity, the heart may develop disturbance or disease.

The body is an amazing creation. You can use it to create whether you are conscious of all of the moving parts doing their job or not. Just as you can drive your car without understanding all about it, you can create through your body without understanding all about it. You can create more effectively and more the way you want by learning to know how your body operates. If you are having problems with your body, look within yourself and relate the body part to your spiritual creativity. You may not be owning your gonads if you are having difficulty creating the survival situation that you want. You may need to get in touch with and learn to express your affinity and control your emotions if you are having heart problems.

There is a long list of examples of how the body reflects you as spirit and how you are creating through your body. The pineal gland relates to your sixth chakra and clairvoyance. It is a reflector of light and of you as spirit. The pituitary gland is the master gland and relates to the seventh chakra or master chakra. The thyroid gland relates to the fifth chakra and communication, both physical and spiritual. You can meditate on any part of your body to learn more about your creative system, your body.

The list goes on. Muscles are associated with movement and strength. If you are having difficulty with flexibility or strength, you could meditate on what interferes with these attributes, clear the interference, and enhance the physical system. The brain relates to the memory and intellect. If you have difficulty remembering something, you can meditate on what you do not want to remember and allow yourself to face your past experiences so you can move forward. The blood is associated with spiritual life force. Jesus talked about the blood of his body as a way of symbolically teaching about the life force of spiritual energy flowing through him. If your circulation is not correct, turn within to your spiritual information and discover what you as spirit need to change to create a healing. You may simply need to pay attention to your body and love it. You may need to change something physical, such as creating an exercise program for yourself or changing your diet. The needed change may relate to emotions, your work or relationship with others. When you meditate on any imbalance in your body, you can find the answer and act on it to heal yourself.

All of the different parts of your body are connected, just as the old song says, "the ankle bone is connected to the leg bone." Reflexology is a healing art that works with energy points in the hands and feet to assist in the release of energy from organs throughout the body. Acupuncture also works with energy points to affect various organs. These healing arts help us see the connectedness of everything in our body and how one action affects everything within it to some extent.

You need to see that you are spirit and your body is your creative expression. Every cell is made by your concepts. Every organ is operated by your beliefs and ideas. You can create your physical reality with a great deal more control by relating to your body and its parts as your spiritual expression. If there is something you do not like, you need to learn about it. You will see if it is something you want to change or something you need to accept as part of your life lesson. Meditation is the easiest way to get to know yourself, your body, and how to work together. Talk to your body. Talk to different parts of your body. If a part is hurt or ill, talk to it to enhance the healing process. Learn about your body and you can use it more effectively.

Your body is your playground and the organs of the body are the different toys. You could imagine your body as your computerized robot and know that everything it does is at your direction, or misdirection as the case may be. You are the creator of the body and the one responsible for all of its actions and experiences. The bones, muscles, skin, internal organs and every part of your body is part of your spiritual creative expression. Love your body and treat it as the temple of God that it is. You can operate in the physical world as the aspect of God that you are when you own your physical temple, the body.

THE ASTRAL BODY:
OUR LIGHTER GARMENT

As spiritual beings on planet Earth we create through matter. We are energy. Since energy and matter are equivalent, we can create form by slowing energy vibrations to create matter. The physical body is one of the forms we create to function within this physical system.

The astral body is a lighter form of the physical body. It is often called the energy body and is not as dense as the physical body. The astral body is within the physical body unless moved out by the soul or by invasion. It can be moved out of the physical body at will and used as a vehicle just as we use the physical body. It looks like the physical body but can be changed at will to look any way the soul wishes. This instant alteration is possible because the astral body is lighter energy than the physical body and is not limited by time.

Both the physical and astral bodies are for use on planet Earth. The astral body and the astral plane are a part of the Earth's energetic system just as much as the physical body and plane. Most people are not conscious of the astral level of Earth since most have given up their spiritual abilities, such as clairvoyance, which allow us to perceive this spiritual level. It is time for people to awaken to this lighter spiritual system and the reality that we have two garments to wear while creating on Earth.

One way people often explain their experiences with the astral body and plane is by calling them "dreams." Many so called "dreams" are actually astral experiences or the soul operating in its astral body outside of the physical body. A dream is actually a cleansing of the body in which mental image pictures, poisons, and other disturbances are being purged from the body. A dream is confusing and does not make logical sense. You do not have a sense of yourself or your body during a dream but of confusing memories or scenes. Dreams usually occur when you have overloaded the body with something. Dreams may occur when you overeat, drink too much alcohol, watch a great deal of television, get too busy with activities or other over indulgences or stimuli. The dream is the body randomly clearing out foreign or disruptive energy.

An astral experience is as real to you as an experience

in your physical body. You can walk, talk, and interact with others while operating in the astral body. Your physical body is asleep during this astral activity unless you are adept enough to operate both your physical and astral bodies at once. The astral body can do everything the physical body can do plus other achievements because of its light composition and its freedom from time and space considerations.

We have both the heavy, dense physical body and the light, ethereal astral body to provide us with two levels of creativity. The physical body is too heavy for us to create on some spiritual levels. The astral body is too light to create effectively on some physical levels. The astral body can function without effort, time or space and the physical body uses all of these energies. The physical body is for experiencing the present moment while the astral body can be used to experience the past and the future. The physical body is bound by gravity because of its density and weight. The astral body is light and can move through space as if it is flying or walking on water.

Spirit is not either body, but the creator of both bodies. Spirit can use either body and can become conscious of all of its experiences in both the physical and astral bodies. Spirit can have the bodies together or separate them. The bodies are together most of the time for the majority of people and separate while the physical body sleeps.

All of the great teachers are adept at using their astral body and operating on the astral plane. Many spiritual teachings were given through an astral body. Jesus used his astral body as effectively as he did his physical body. He often was seen operating in his astral body as he could manifest his energy body as strongly as he could his physical body. There are many references to Jesus presenting himself in his astral body throughout the New Testament of the Christian Bible. There are also folk tales from different parts of the world about visits from Jesus. One story is of a holy man who floated down the Columbia River telling the local tribe to be peaceful and give up war. The holy man is identified as Jesus. There are many such stories about Jesus' astral body visits to different groups around the world.

You do not have to be a great teacher to use your astral body. Anyone can learn to remember this level of spiritual creativity. You can start by remembering your astral experiences that occur while your body sleeps. An easy way to open your awareness to the astral level is to write down anything you remember when you awaken from sleep during the night or in the morning. Eventually you can learn to remember your astral experiences as clearly as your physical life.

Many life issues are worked out on the astral plane. Most souls test possible futures in the lighter astral body before creating it in the denser physical reality. When I first met my husband, Doc, we were both students in a spiritual program. I had always been aware of my astral experiences and could describe them in detail. When Doc teased me about visiting him every night in my astral body I was embarrassed and denied the visits, since we were just flirting at that stage of our courtship. He caught me at my game by asking me what color his sheets were and I immediately said, "white, but they were flowered till last night." He laughed, since I so quickly admitted my interest in him, and informed me I was correct as he had changed his sheets the day before.

We use our astral body to work on future relationships such as my flirtation with my husband which turned out to be very successful. We also use it to work out emotional relationships that we do not want to face in the physical body. Whether we deal with past or future, we can test and work on many creative ideas before we materialize them in our physical world.

The astral body can be used any place in the Earth in an instant as it is lighter and closer to the vibration of spiritual energy. We do not have the time, space, mass, and effort limits for the astral body that we have for the physical body. We can lay the physical body down and travel anywhere on Earth in the astral body to perform any type of interaction.

My husband had to take a nap one morning and had an astral experience with my father who was dying. Doc experienced helping my father find his way to a freeway where he would have a straight road to his destination. After Doc woke up, we were having lunch and received a telephone call from my sister saying my father had died at the exact time Doc was helping him on the astral plane. It was a joy to know that my father had loving assistance in his transition out of his body.

We live on the West Coast and my family lives on the East Coast. We as spirit have the astral body to use when the physical body cannot accomplish the task for us.

The astral body is a wonderful aspect of our earthly creativity to wake up to and learn to use. We can use it to communicate, experiment, heal and create. We can use it to become more spiritually aware and competent in this earthly reality. The astral body helps us be aware of our immortality as spirit. It allows us to create as the powerful beings we are. The astral body does not die like the physical body. We can learn to maintain it to use in the Earth reality after the death of the physical body if this is our path.

The astral body is what people are seeing when they claim to see a ghost. It is the shimmering of energy caused by the manifestation of an astral body. It may be someone without a physical body or a very capable being able to manifest its astral body enough to be seen. If the soul has enough power, it can manifest its astral body sufficiently to move objects or to be seen.

Astral bodies can be programmed just as physical bodies can, so it is important to learn to own and clear your astral body as well as your physical body. I suggest you begin with learning to clear your physical body and then meditate on clearing the astral body. Grounding is a very important technique to master before you begin experimenting with your astral body. Grounding is described in the chapter on Spiritual Techniques. When you are ready to meditate on the astral body, you will need to learn about your third chakra.[3] The third chakra contains information on out-of-body memory and out-of-body experience. Meditation is essential in mastering the astral body.

The astral body and the astral plane can be used as a powerful spiritual healing level. Waking up to this lighter aspect of your spiritual creativity can add an exciting and beneficial dimension to your life. Let yourself see that there is more on Earth than the physically obvious.

INNER SPACE:
SPIRIT CREATING THROUGH MATTER

The physical body and the energy around it are the inner space to be explored and used by the soul. Turning within is the way to discover yourself. Through the physical body, the soul creates and learns. When the soul knows itself, it knows everything. The great teachers all say "know yourself." This self knowledge is imperative to spiritual evolvement and enlightenment.

Everything is within you. All your questions, answers, and information are within you or can be accessed through you. You can learn everything you need to know by tuning into yourself. You can give everything you are here to share by working from within yourself. You cannot accomplish your spiritual or even your physical goals outside yourself. This inner space is your body and the area surrounding your body called your aura. You are meant to create through this space. If you do not, you are floating through the physical life without a home.

Your body is your vehicle to create, communicate, and evolve on Earth. You must learn how to use it and operate through it in order to accomplish your spiritual purpose. Whether your purpose is to develop the body to the level that you can leave it and work outside it, as some yoga masters do, or develop it to allow you to move as fully as possible through your body, you must begin to focus within.

In a practical sense anyone can see the logic of operating within one's personal space. If you are outside your body you are not as focused or aware of the physical reality as when you are inside or focused on your body. You may think of this as "day dreaming" or fantasizing instead of being out of your body. Either way, you are not focused. Remember how little you retained in class if you "day dreamed." Whether you are operating machinery, baking a cake, teaching children, playing a sport, meditating, or functioning in any way in this world, it is helpful to be aware of your body. If you are not aware of your body, you are not in charge of what is happening in your reality.

Recently I was running and made the mistake of leaving my body to focus on a healing project relating to someone else. Immediately I fell and hurt my knee and frightened my body. The remainder of the morning I focused my attention on myself where it belonged. By focusing in the present moment in our personal space, we are focused on our creativity in matter. I was focusing on someone else's creativity and paid the price of losing control of my body and letting it get hurt. This simple example shows how we can get off track or even harm ourselves by not focusing within.

The inner focus keeps you in touch with the present moment of your physical reality. What is happening now? How do you want to respond to what is occurring? What are your beliefs and how do you want to use them in this circumstance? Life is an endless opportunity to make decisions and choices. These choices create your reality. Do you know what you believe about a given situation? Do you know who you are? Are you operating as spirit or allowing your body to create its own reality without your guidance?

Your body is a composite of your beliefs and experiences as spirit. You manifest yourself through these beliefs. You are in charge of your creativity when you are aware of what you are doing. You may discover a belief you accepted from a parent that you want to change or one you brought from a past life that is no longer appropriate. If you are not focused in your space, you will not be aware that a belief is causing you difficulty and will look outside for the cause. This outer focus will confuse you more as the correct information for you is within you. By working with your body, you learn through your experience of being on Earth.

You can educate yourself from the wealth of information around you, but you must eventually turn to yourself for your way of operating. Parental training, peer group pressure, teachers, and all of the outside influences in life are not responsible for your actions. You are responsible for all of your behavior. You need to learn how to turn within to discover what is correct for you. This level of personal responsibility brings you physical and spiritual maturity.

Every soul needs its personal space to create. Our personal space is a God-given gift to allow each of us to develop to our level of capability. We each need our space to express our spiritual vibration and nature and learn what we need to develop. Without our space we do not have the correct information for our specific development. We need space to grow just as a tree needs space to grow to its full height. We become spiritually stunted if we do not have space to function.

You have to own your space to have it. You have to decide what you will have within your space. While your body is a fetus, you determine what you will internalize from your mother. When you are born, you decide what experiences to take on to function through in life. During all of your developmental stages you monitor what you will keep and what you will let go of. You decide what agreements to make and which ones to fulfill and which ones to discard. You are the creator of your reality as you determine what you will use and what you will release. If you believe that you are a victim to your surroundings and to others, then you will be, as you create from your beliefs. You will also

Just as your view of life changes from childhood to adulthood, so your perspective changes as spirit when you grow to a new level of awareness. You are not a static energy. You are spirit and you are constantly changing and growing.

absorb a great deal that you do not need or want because of this belief. You are in charge and need to know this. By changing your beliefs you change your life.

You as spirit need to pay attention to your creative process from beginning to end, in order to create what you want. From conception to death you are continuing to learn and grow in your body, as you create and destroy concepts and pictures which make up your physical manifestation. You are the one who determines what you keep and what you destroy. This process allows you to heal and grow. Just as your view of life changes from childhood to adulthood, so your perspective changes as spirit when you grow to a new level of awareness. You are not a static energy. You are spirit and you are constantly changing and growing.

Your beliefs are your physical building bricks in this evolutionary process. You can build with your beliefs or ones that you accepted from other souls or from the collective consciousness of society. You may believe that tall people are beautiful because you were taught that. If you have a tall body, you believe you are beautiful. You may have a short body and punish your body your entire life because of this belief. The next life you would probably create a tall body because you prayed for one the last life. You could end up in a short society and feel unattractive again. You need to be aware of you as spirit to fulfill your spiritual needs instead of attempting to fulfill the ideals of the society.

You need to turn within to your spiritual vibration,

purpose and beliefs to know your way of operating in the physical world. This inward focus will allow you to see yourself. You will see what is yours that you want to use and what you wish to clear. You will see what you have accepted from others that you want to keep and what you want to release. You will see yourself as you are and can make any necessary adjustments to create what you need to fulfill your present life goals.

You learn why you have created certain strengths and weaknesses when you look within and know yourself. You can see that they are for your education. You need certain strengths to accomplish your goals and certain weaknesses to learn your lessons. By turning within to your inner space you get to know yourself. You are certainly the most interesting person to you, so this process is fascinating.

You own this inner space by taking responsibility for it. You acknowledge that every thought, belief, and experience is yours while in your space. Whether you created or adopted the concept, it is yours while it is in your space. You then determine whether you want the idea or not. If you do want the belief, you can own it as yours regardless of its origin. If you do not want the belief, you can clear it from your space.

Knowing yourself and using your inner space is the spiritual process you must pursue to consciously evolve through a life. You can compare owning your inner space to the territorial behavior of animals. An animal knows its territory, what is in it, how to get around in it, how best to utilize it. He owns it from other animals so he can use it for himself. You have to do the same with your body and your body space. If you do not, you will not create for yourself but for someone else.

There are many situations where people go to a school, marry someone, develop a profession, or live in a particular place because their parents want them to. This is an example of not owning your personal space. You can love and respect others while living your purpose in life instead of theirs. You may have the experience of trying to look like the models in magazines or the actors on television. This is another example of not owning your inner space. You are trying to be like someone else instead of manifesting your unique vibration and concepts.

Clearing your space of unwanted debris is a process that allows you to manifest yourself and own your inner space. The more you move out what you do not want, the more you can move your unique energy into your body. The more you are in your body and creating through it, the less energy you have for focusing on things outside of you. You become responsive to the world around you instead of trying to change the world to comply with the confusion you have in your space.

Present time is another way of focusing in your inner space. You can be aware of what is happening within and around you when you are in the present. Your body can help you learn to focus in the present. You can listen to your heart beat and your breathing to bring your attention back to the moment. Your power and creativity are in the present.

You can learn to know yourself in the present as you are dealing with what is occurring at the moment, not what happened in the past or what will happen in the future. If you discover something that is not in the present, you can clear it from your space. You do not have to be controlled by past experiences or future desires. You can experience the universe within you in the present.

By taking responsibility for your body and your creativity through it, being in the present and clearing what you do not want or need from this space, you can create fully within your personal space. This is an exciting experience as you are the master of your creativity. You are in charge of your body and everything you do through it. You know that you create through your beliefs instead of foreign or inappropriate beliefs. You can easily see when you take on something that you do not want or create something that you do not want to keep.

You create new things to choose from along the way, so the process of cleansing does not end as you continue to move through the matter of physical existence. The clarity you develop by operating through your inner space makes it easier for you to see what is happening. When you drive your car with a dirty windshield, you cannot see where you are going. If you try to reach a destination without correct directions, you will get lost. By focusing within, you know who you are and where you are going and can see to get there.

You lose your space when you allow another soul to

create through your system or when you try to create through another soul's system. You have to allow others to have their personal space in order to maintain your inner space. You may think about your space like a house. If you are not at home, others can come into your house and use it. They may leave it a mess or destroy some part of it. You may have been at someone else's house, trying to change it and return to your house to find it disturbed. You were unable to create what you wanted in the other house and allowed your house to be invaded because you were not paying attention to it. Your house or your space is where you are meant to create.

You may know someone who is constantly telling everyone else what to do. They have their attention outside of their space in everyone else's space. This soul will have difficulty fulfilling its goals as there is no inner focus to create what it wants. People who are so outwardly focused are attempting to create their reality through someone else's body. This does not work and causes frustration for everyone concerned. Each soul is meant to create through its own body. Such an outward focus is usually caused by disturbance in the inner space that is being denied or ignored. If the body is filled with pain or hate, the soul will look for a more comfortable space through which to create. This leaves its body empty and vulnerable to invasion and does not accomplish its creative goals, as a soul cannot effectively create through another's body.

You need to maintain your energy within your space to create what you are here on Earth to do. You also find your information within your space. The physical and spiritual systems are set up for you to create through them. By floating around or invading the space of others, you waste your energy and disrupt the energy around you. Everyone needs to create through his or her own beliefs and energy. To do this, we must operate through our personal space.

Our inner space is a world of excitement and creative entertainment. There is no possibility for boredom when one is tuned into this inner space. We can access everything from a single cell to the Cosmos through our personal space. We can experience more through this space than through any man made devices, such as television, movies or entertainment parks. While our external entertainment can be fun, our internal experience is of the greatest value.

Our inner frontier contains all we have learned over many lifetimes. We can access Cosmic Consciousness through our inner space. We can talk to world teachers and God within this inner space. We can sit in a room in our home and communicate with anyone, anywhere in the world. We can experience our spiritual power and autonomy within our space. We can know the world by knowing ourselves.

God has given you inner personal space to experiment with your creativity. It is your personal laboratory. Your inner space is yours to create within and through. No one else has the right to create within your space unless you allow it. You are the god within your personal space, deciding everything that occurs. You are the master of this space and are senior to all other spirit within this personal space. Your inner space is your home, your vessel, your clothing, for a lifetime. It belongs to you and needs to be owned and kept clear for you to function to your fullest capability.

You create your state of being. It is necessary for you to own your space to create the state you wish. You create your happiness or sadness and how you use your energy and space. Nothing outside of you creates your state of being. You are the creator of your reality. You can experience joy in a seemingly unpleasant environment. You can be miserable in the midst of abundance and pleasure. Your emotional state, energetic state, and conscious expression are under your control if you focus within yourself. External stimuli do not have to affect you to the extent that most people allow.

A graphic example of this is a woman I knew who was looking for a man who could provide her with sexual satisfaction. She was a beautiful young woman with a great deal of sexual appeal. She attracted men but could not create a relationship because none of the men could perform what she wanted. This sexual satisfaction had to come from within her, not from someone outside of her. She did not have the correct beliefs to create sexual satisfaction. She had been abused, and her sexual concepts were associated with pain instead of pleasure. She spent most of her time looking for this illusive satisfaction outside of herself instead of looking within to clear the barriers to her personal creativity.

Another example of attempting to create outside personal space is a very capable man who is seeking his spiritual information from books, seminars, tapes, and various teachers without internalizing or owning any of the information. He has a great deal of personal power and ability, yet he does not use the spiritual teachings within his personal space to enhance his spiritual growth. He tries to use the information outside his body, since his body is filled with his childhood religious programming and painful childhood memories. Because his vessel, the body, is already full of other energy, as spirit he sits above his body and uses only the intellect and upper chakras to deal with the information. He refuses to take time to cleanse his body to receive the spiritual information and continues to relate to the spiritual realm through his intellect. He is locked in a continuous external search for himself as he refuses to turn within and face what he has stored in his body, clear it, and move into the body as his home.

You as spirit can experience and create all you are here on Earth to do through your inner space. Meditation is the easiest way to learn about your space and how to use and control it. You learn in much the same way the body learns. You begin by planting the idea of you into matter, growing the idea, and birthing it into the material world. You learn how the body works and how to use it. You learn about time and space, energy, mass, gravity, effort, competition, emotions, sexuality, and all of the body phenomena. You learn how to interact with things outside your personal space and how to navigate your way through existing reality. You learn what beliefs you can keep and what beliefs you have to destroy to survive, create and thrive.

You create your reality through what you brought with you and what you learned thus far in this lifetime. Most souls are not taught to look within to this inner space and must relearn the necessity of an inner focus in adulthood. This requires changes in your belief system if you were taught to look outside yourself for information. Once you look within and discover that you are spirit, it is easy and fun to create from your personal space.

This inner level of spiritual creativity is what we are here to learn. Everything we need is found within. Our energy, knowledge, information, and our relationship with God and all things are found within. We can interact with the world from our armchair or go out into the world to create. Either way, everything is found within our space. If you like someone, look within and you will find what you like in yourself also. If you do not like someone, look within and you will discover the same traits within you. You can own what you like and destroy what you do not like. The key is that everything is within you.

The body and the spiritual system within and around it are our personal space ship on Earth. This system is our control room and our ship through life. By learning to run it and use it for our spiritual purpose, we fulfill our mission on planet Earth. Whether we are here to travel and do, or sit at home and be, our vehicle in which to do it is our body and inner space.

You as spirit create your body to function in the material world. You have the right to create whatever you want in your personal space. You have the right to be happy or sad, rich or poor, creative or not. You can create a desert or a garden within your space.

We are collectively using planet Earth as our space in the larger Universe. Individually we have our body to experience the collective space and together we have the body of Earth to experience the larger cosmic space. We are learning to work with time, space, mass and other physical concepts as we learn our lessons in creation through matter. By owning and fully using our individual bodies, we do our part for the collective consciousness and our planet. Each part effectively used makes up a harmonious whole.

COMMUNICATING ON EARTH

We communicate and create through our main manifestation on Earth, our body. We create, learn and communicate by manipulating our energy through our body and through the environment of Earth. Communication is the most interactive aspect of our creativity. We communicate in everything we do. Every action of our body is a communication. Every thought, deed, emotion, and word is a form of communication. Communication is an important form of spiritual creativity, and it is an aspect of love.

Your movements, thoughts, emotions, words, and deeds all communicate you to the world around you. The body language of stance and movement expresses a great deal to others. You show whether you are aggressive or passive, friendly or harmful, happy or sad, and many other states of consciousness. What are you saying about yourself when you stand on one foot? What do you express when you stand firmly on both feet? What do you communicate with your hands on your hips or your hands in your pockets? Every gesture is a communication. When you realize how many gestures you make in a few minutes, you learn how much you are saying with your body movements.

The entire body is a communication system. Its movements express us as spirit and the emotions of the body. Body language is a type of communication used by all animals including humans. The turn of a head, wink of an eye, wave of a hand say a great deal. The body's expression of nervousness or calm indicate the state of the being in the body and the experience of the body. We are constantly communicating to the world through our bodies.

Words are our most commonly accepted and acknowledged way of communicating. Language enhances communication for the body and gives more energy and power to the physical level. Words in spoken and written form have a great deal of energy just as all physical things have energy. Once you have spoken a word, you have created a vibration. Do you remember wishing you could withdraw a statement? Once spoken, the energy is there.

Words are a low vibration of energy compared to telepathy, clairaudience, and other non-verbal communications. I enjoy using words because they are a vibration that reaches most people. Some people attempt to create their entire reality through words. This can be fun but it does limit one's creativity to the physical plane as words are a physical manifestation. I have known people who talk constantly in an attempt to control their environment. It may be fascinating for them, but they do not learn much about the world around them. They are probably afraid and use words to protect themselves.

Some words have more energy invested in them than others. Some energy is originated by society and some by the concept the word represents. The most energy packed word is "God." Probably the second most emotionally loaded word is "love." These words have so much energy tied up in them that few people are neutral about either of them. Words vary in the amount of energy vested in them.

You have varying amounts and types of energy invested in different words depending on your life experience. Not all the energy is correct for the meaning of the word because of the experiences you have had when hearing the word. For example, a child may be slapped when hearing the words, "Jesus, you make me mad." The child then has the energy of pain and anger tied into the word "Jesus" as well as the other concepts he has learned in church. He will feel confused and angry about the word "Jesus" until he clears the energy collected through pain.

Words have power. We have given the written word inordinate power. Many people believe that if something is in print it is correct. This interferes with the natural process of looking within for your own information. Words are the form we use to communicate from one body to another body. We also have learned to use words within ourselves. We sometimes have difficulty turning the words off to listen to our spiritual communication since our lives are inundated with words.

It does help to realize how much power words have. You can then be aware of what you are creating by using words. You can be more aware of what you are doing to your environment when you are conscious of the power of words. You can decide how you want to create your world through your communication. What do you want to say to others? What vibration do you want to create? You can use words to attract and to repel others. You can use words to create a great deal of your physical environment.

It is helpful to neutralize your relationship with words. You can meditate on words that have a lot of energy for you or have foreign energy or pain in them. This way you can take control of words and how you use them. What words mean more to you than the commonly accepted meaning? You can clear the unwanted energy and have a neutral relationship with the word. You can also learn to see how words affect others. If you have a friend react strangely to something ordinary that you say, you can understand that it may not be your communication but one word in your statement. If your friend had experienced pain around the word "Jesus," he might have an angry reaction to an otherwise unemotional communication.

Since everything in the physical reality is a potential avenue for communication, the avenue of words needs to be accepted for the power that it has. We gain control of this aspect of our power by acknowledging it as a powerful manifestation of energy into matter. Words are a way we communicate and create in a body. We can learn to own, clear and use words in a spiritual manner and have a great deal of fun working and playing with them.

Deeds are another way we communicate through our body. What we do often speaks louder than words. We all know someone who speaks in a gruff manner and seldom has kind words, but who is always helping others. The gruffness is a facade to protect this healer. If we look beyond the facade of words, we see the true manifestation of the healer. The opposite can also be true where someone speaks sweet words and acts in a hateful manner. The actions are the stronger manifestation when the words and deeds do not match.

Your deeds speak loudly about you and what you believe. What are you doing in your life? Are your deeds communicating what you want to say to others? Do you believe that your deeds do not matter? Everything you do creates a vibration on Earth. If you do what you as spirit are here to create, you manifest a spiritual message. If you operate as a body, you communicate a physical message. What you do expresses you to the world.

Unfortunately, much of the world is accustomed to a facade of words instead of the reality of deeds. Deeds require more energy, time, and commitment than words. As the old saying goes, "Words are cheap." If you want to do something, you have to go through the steps to make it manifest physically. If you want to build a house, you must collect the building materials, create a plan, and then do the work to carry out the plan. This takes time, energy, and commitment. Talking about building a house takes much less energy and commitment than building one. You can talk forever without actually doing anything.

You can learn a great deal about yourself and what you are communicating to the world by looking at your deeds. You are creating your reality with your actions. You are communicating your beliefs through the deeds you perform. If you do not like your performance, you can change it. You can meditate on your deeds and decide what you wish to change. You can then heal your communication to the world by changing the deeds you perform in this world. You can create love instead of hate. You can use power instead of weakness. You can communicate spirit in all of your deeds.

Your deeds are a strong way to communicate your personal vibration to the physical world. If you believe life has no meaning, then your deeds will have little meaning to you. If you believe that you are spirit and are here on Earth for a purpose, then your deeds will have a great deal of meaning to you. You need to evaluate your deeds to determine what you want. Your deeds communicate you.

Thoughts are another form of communication. Every thought you have is a physical manifestation. You may say that you like someone, but think that you hate them. The thought will be the more powerful manifestation and will be the loudest communication to the receiver. When you think something, it becomes real in the physical world. You may not manifest it immediately, but you will eventually make it happen if you do not destroy the thought form.

Thoughts manifest physically in this reality. Just as you planted the idea of you through conception, you plant energy with every thought. You think, "I want to go to Hawaii." You say, "I want to go to Hawaii." You perform going to Hawaii. The thought is the most subtle form of communication of the three and requires less energy than words or deeds. Thoughts are just as real as the other forms of communication. In fact, the other two are always preceded by the thought. Thought is similar to conception as the thought plants the seed.

Physical communication is similar to physical manifestation. First there is the thought, then the word, then the deed, each stage requiring more energy and commitment to accomplish. Thoughts are the most subtle of our communications; thus they are one of the most tempting to play with and the least owned. Most people do not believe that their thoughts have power. Thoughts do have power and energy. Our thoughts are the planting of an idea. We then grow and birth the idea, or we destroy it. Too often we forget to destroy unwanted thoughts, and they manifest in the future as a surprise.

I had to stop and spend the night in a motel between my home and Spokane, Washington, not long ago, and I wondered why I had created that. The next morning I remembered that I had once before passed by the motel while tired and formed the thought that I would like to stay there - it was so attractive. The next day I spent a few hours destroying thoughts that were no longer appropriate or in the present.

When we think something, we have created it. We do not have to let it grow or manifest it in most cases, but often the thought is all we need to make it manifest without doing anything further. We are not taught to be aware of our thoughts. In fact, we are usually taught that our thoughts are private and cannot hurt others. There is not one thing in spiritual reality that is private. There is only the illusion of privacy. Our thoughts affect us and our world. Thoughts create energy and energy affects all other energy.

When you think of someone else, they receive the energy of your thoughts. They may even receive the experience of your reality if you focus your thoughts on them strongly enough and they are a good receiver. During a visit to Hawaii, I was acutely aware of my niece and my secretary thinking of me and wanting to be with me on vacation. They were so focused on me that at times it seemed they were there with me. I kept sending them the thought to call on the phone as that would allow me more personal space for my vacation. Unless you want someone to know you very well, be cautious with your thoughts. A less pleasant experience of receiving someone else's thoughts was receiving a message of fury and hate from a staff member who was upset with changes in her life that she believed I helped generate. She projected her thoughts at me, and I experienced her state of being. I telephoned her to talk about this, and she responded, "Oh, you really do hear me!" We hear and experience each other's thoughts consciously or unconsciously. I encourage everyone to become conscious of communication in order to respond realistically.

An aspect of our thoughts are our fantasies. Our fantasies are also forms of energy and will eventually manifest in physical form unless destroyed. Our fantasies of this life will become the reality of the next life if we do not destroy those thought forms. Those innocent or not so innocent fantasies have greater meaning and power than most people believe. They are energy manifested in matter.

Evaluate your fantasies and make sure they are truly what you want to create as they will eventually be your reality. The fantasy may not manifest exactly as you imagined, as other fantasies and creations will combine with it and you may be in a different body and physical setting. You could be like the man living in a bad dream of sexual promiscuity and abuse because he fantasized about it in a previous life. If you grow to the point where you no longer like your fantasies, you can take your energy out of them and not manifest them. The point is that your fantasies are a communication of you to the world and will be part of your creative process if you continue to put energy into them or forget to destroy them.

As spirit, all your communications have power and physical implications. Even if the communication is not verbalized or acted out, it still has physical energy and impact. You may be thinking that you cannot keep up with every thought and fantasy, but you can. You can learn to be in control of your communication and your creativity. It may take you years to do this, but you will then be in charge of your communication in the physical world. You can learn about your communication through meditation and an inward focus.

Our emotions are another way we communicate. Our body talks to us and to other bodies through emotions. Most people are taught to use emotions for communication with others instead of paying attention to their own emotions. The more important communication is from body to spirit. When spirit knows what is happening with the body, it can be in charge of communication and its physical creativity.

Emotional communication to others lets them know the emotional state of your body. This can be helpful for those living closely together and needing to know what is happening in their environment. You do not need to project your emotions onto others. They can receive the message more easily if you do not put too much energy behind the emotional message. If you do project the emotion, you may overwhelm the other person. You then wonder why they are not responding and send more emotional energy. This overdose of your emotional energy will probably not get you the results you want. It usually pushes the other person away from you instead of attracting them.

We do need to realize when we communicate with emotions that we are projecting our body energy and it does not work in anyone else's space. We are clearer in our communication if we as spirit listen to the body's emotional message and then relate it in a more neutral fashion to others. This is difficult in the case of fear or fury, but we can learn to be in control of our emotional communications. Control of this level of communication requires paying attention to the body and working with it.

We as spirit communicate in many ways that are less body-oriented. We communicate telepathically, clairaudiently, with mental image pictures, symbols and with our inner voice. Telepathy is the ability to send messages without speaking. We do this any time we have a thought about another person. We send the message as we have the thought. We may say, "How nice to see you" and think, "Not you again." The receiver will get the second message as well as the first one.

Telepathy is a communication skill you can have fun experimenting with. You and a friend can send each other messages and record them to compare later. You may be surprised how often you connect and both have the same or a similar message. You may have experienced this form of communication with a child or in an emergency. You may have experienced telepathy from your mate to buy something at the store and gotten home to discover their delight that you bought just what they wanted you to. Animals are capable telepaths. You can have fun communicating with pets telepathically, and they appreciate being acknowledged.

Clairaudience is the ability to communicate with beings that do not have physical bodies, such as angels, and over long distances. It can save a lot on telephone bills. Telephones are a physical manifestation of telepathy and clairaudience. You can learn to communicate with friends who are far away. You can also learn to communicate with your spiritual guides. This communication with guides can expand your awareness to a new spiritual level. Clairaudience allows you to communicate with spiritual guides without letting them into your body space.

You do not have to allow another soul into your space to communicate with them. You can use your clairaudient channels to speak with spirit and allow both your space and theirs. You can become conscious of your communications and be in charge of them. You are meant to have your body and space and not to share it with another being. Your clairaudient channels allow you to have all the communication with spirit that you want without losing your space to have it.

As spirit, we store our information in the form of mental image pictures, symbols, and formulas. We can use these to communicate with other souls. We put the mental image picture of a house out to another soul to send that message. The picture of something is a single thing. A symbol and a formula represent broader concepts or a larger picture. We can communicate what we believe through a symbol or formula as well as through pictures. Every spirit is a mathematician since symbols and formulas are a favorite form of spiritual communication. These formulas and symbols show others who we are as spirit and what we have accomplished.

Because we communicate through and with them, pictures are very important in our communication and creativity through the body. We need to be aware of the pictures within our system. If we have a picture that other people are loving, then we will create through that. If we believe that other people are dangerous, then we will create and communicate through that concept. Our entire system is made up of our pictures, so we always communicate through these pictures.

The abuse issues that are being brought into people's awareness are an example of how we create through pictures. If a woman is abused as a child by her father, she has the pictures of pain and fear associated with child care and parent-child interactions. When she becomes a parent she will create and communicate through those pictures of pain and fear unless she clears them from her space. If she has a male child she may act out her experiences in his system and thus give him the same pictures through which to create. He then, in turn, will pass the experiences on to his child. The pictures become self perpetuating unless a soul stops the pattern by clearing the pictures. One does not have to act out the thought or picture for someone else to be affected by it. The abusive perspective can be taught through concepts, beliefs, and emotions.

Mental image pictures are major aspects of our

communication. We need to see the pictures we have, so we know what we are communicating. Our body and energy system are created of our spiritual pictures, so we are communicating through a system of beliefs. We can change our system, including our way of communicating, by changing a single picture. We can clear abuse pictures and end abusive behavior. This takes time and discipline and can be accomplished through dedicated meditation.

Mental image pictures help us recognize one another as spirit even from previous lives. We are able to know immediately who another being is and what they believe as spirit. It usually takes us some time to bring this information into the conscious awareness of the body. We need to learn how to communicate clearly with our body so the spiritual awareness can translate to the body quickly. In this way, we know whether we want to associate with another being or not. We recognize if the interaction is a beneficial learning opportunity or a detour on our spiritual journey.

The inner voice is part of the spirit-body communication system. This inner voice sounds just like the voice of your body. Talking to yourself is necessary for you to know what is happening for you as both spirit and body. You as spirit need to know what is occurring for the body so you can relate to your physical creativity. Your body needs to hear the communication from you to understand what you are doing through it. If you are creating a learning experience through your body without informing the body, it will be afraid, confused, or angry. If you are creating through your body without listening to it, you can get off track by not knowing what is happening in the physical setting.

An example of the need for spirit-body communication is a friend of mine who wanted to get pregnant. Her body was focused on the physical act of conception. It was also invaded by other people telling her to hurry up because she was getting close to an age when pregnancy would be difficult if not impossible to create. She was not listening to herself as spirit or to the being for whom she was creating the body. Both she and the other spirit were aware when the conception would occur, but the body was not hearing because of the invasion from others and her focus on intellectual perspectives. She was afraid, upset, and confused. After she was assisted to get in touch with the being for whom she was creating the body, she learned that the conception would occur in a few months. This relieved her, but she continued to be afraid until the baby was conceived since she had not developed her inner voice and her belief in herself as spirit.

You can change your life a great deal by opening your communication between yourself as spirit and your body. Both levels of your creativity benefit as each area knows what is occurring in the other arena. You learn to believe in yourself and your power to create what you need, as you talk to yourself and reassure, educate, and inform yourself about what is being created. Your inner voice is your direct communication with you as spirit which is the aspect of God within you.

Communication is one of the greatest joys for spirit. We revel in the excitement of communication on every level. We can learn to gain a great deal of control over our communication whether it is with self or others. We can learn to turn off what we do not want and turn up what we want to enhance. Communication is very important to our creativity on Earth.

Pay attention to yourself, to your body, and to what others are really saying and you will discover a world of entertainment and education in your life. You can communicate as spirit in the physical world. You can learn to communicate with all living things as you open to the wealth of communication available to you in this world. You can learn to communicate spiritually with the great teachers, with your friends, with planet Earth, and with God.

You can talk directly to God at any time or place. Your communication with God can become a part of your daily life. You can incorporate this communion into every thought, word, and deed. Saying a blessing over your food before you eat, praying to or thinking of God before you sleep, asking God's advice through the day are all ways to incorporate God into your life. Recognizing yourself and all others as part of God is another way you can bring your communication with God into your life.

Spirit in matter is meant to be in touch with the Cosmic Consciousness. Bodies are structured for this communication. We need to remember we are spirit, and the body is a communication device so we can reestablish our direct line with God. God is always present; we need to reconnect.

EARTH ANGELS AND DEVILS

Those of us manifesting our energy in a body are not the only souls relating to planet Earth. There are souls who are here to help us in our creative process and souls who want to interfere with this process. Any soul relating to planet Earth must relate to dichotomies or opposites. Thus we have what are commonly called angels and devils. Neither of these are like the stereotypes usually given.

Angels have received a great deal of publicity lately. Since the energy on planet Earth is increasing, the angels are able to communicate more easily with humans. There are many stories of angel interventions in the lives of individuals. This is encouraging as it indicates that people are becoming more spiritually aware and more receptive to spiritual experiences.

Angels are spirits aligned with God. They usually do not have physical bodies but can appear to have a body to make it easier to communicate with those of us who do have bodies. Angels do not interfere in anyone's life unless asked for help. They are always available to help when we request assistance. There are angels beyond counting in physical terms. There are also many types of angels. The important thing is to remember that they do exist and are here to help us if we just ask.

Many people have a personal angel because they asked for help at some time. Children often ask for angelic assistance and then keep a helper with them through life. Small children are especially aware of angels as they do not have the intellectual barriers of doubt and fear we create in later life. Angels are with us; we need to open our awareness to see and communicate with them.

Angels do not have bodies, so they are not bound by the limits of a body. They are free of time, space, mass, effort, pain, competition, and the other physical attributes of a body. They are spirit and in alignment with God. They are here in the Earth plane to help those of us in bodies. Being in a body is a major challenge, and we need all the help we can get.

Angels do not have wings. The wings were painted on pictures of angels years ago to indicate their ability to fly or move through space. Since everyone is intellectually oriented, the belief that angels have wings stuck to explain why they can fly. Angels do not need wings as they do not have mass to move. They are able to appear and disappear at will on the physical plane. They can manipulate their reality in the Earth plane without the limits of a physical body. They use what is often called an energy body to appear to humans. The energy body can function in the world without being subject to its limits.

Some people have seen someone they know as an angel, such as a deceased relative or friend. This is possible. A spirit can leave the physical world and enter service in the angelic world quickly if that spirit is ready to do so. The many levels of angelic hierarchy allows for many souls to move into service easily. The life of the soul on Earth determines the next step and it could be service to those remaining in bodies.

I communicate with angels on a continuing basis. This is possible for anyone who chooses to do so. One incident in childhood stands out as a miraculous encounter. I was in the second grade in school and playing on the school grounds. There was a construction site we were told to avoid. Being a curious and stubborn child I went straight for the area. I walked along some logs and fell about twelve feet down a stairwell into a basement entrance. I landed flat on my back on a concrete floor. I stood up and walked up the incline to the playground. My friends ran for the teacher who would not believe I fell that far since I was now moving. We finally convinced the adults the accident had occurred, and my father came to take me to the doctor. My only injury was a minor concussion to the head.

The only thing I remember about the fall, from the time just before falling until I gained consciousness lying on the concrete floor, was light hands under me. In later life as I looked spiritually at the incident, I saw angels holding my body as much as their light bodies allowed. When I first saw this, I cried with relief to realize that such help is there for any of us and that I finally allowed myself to see the helpers. There are several such incidents in my life when I came close to death and was saved by angelic intervention. I have always known that there is a mission to my life, and I finally realized that I needed to get on with it and use the angels in a more productive manner than saving my body over and over.

Since my childhood and youth, angels have moved from saving my body to telling me about my need to write books and other important information in my life. I have visitations from Gabriel and Michael whenever there is an important change about to occur in my life. I have moved from a childhood dependence on these beings to a more adult interaction of conscious communication.

The nature of angels is as unclear to most people as the fact that they do not need wings. Angels display a level of neutrality that does not compute in our world of intellect and emotion. They will not be sympathetic or try to prove anything. They are there as neutral observers and helpers for us to call on when we are spiritually aware or desperate enough to do so. The fact that angels do not have the same emotional make up as humans confuses many people and causes others to try to make them like humans. They are not bound by human reality and have no physical ties. They are simply helping God by assisting us in our growth process on Earth.

The level of angels relating to Earth varies from what some call nature spirits to divas and archangels. The nature spirits are associated with plants, animals and other aspects of nature. Divas are angels who relate to a particular part of the Earth. Pele is an angel who cares for the Hawaiian Islands. Pele helps us see that angels are not the stereotype usually portrayed of angels. There is also a diva for Mount Saint Helens in Washington State. Most people would not consider it angelic to associate with a volcano which erupted. Angels have a different perspective of reality than humans and do the best they can to help us regain our own spiritual perspective of life on Earth.

What we may perceive as a tragedy or mistake can be used as a freeing experience. The angels see the big picture while we only see part of it. Mount Saint Helens at first appears a disaster, but in the long range view is seen as a way of renewing the Earth. This change brings new soil, atmospheric changes and countless other healing elements. Pele and her volcanic creations are constantly building up land above the sea. Seen from the eyes of someone who had their house buried, eruptions do not appear to be angelically associated, yet these earthly phenomena are spiritually guided.

Angels deal with the magnificent and the mundane.

They help with a child in need of a friend or the issues of planetary transformation. Angels are in tune with God so nothing is too large or too small for their attention. They can help us through any life change or circumstance and are always available to help us bring our attention back to the spiritual realm and God.

Anyone can communicate with angels. Meditation can help you prepare your system to talk with angels. You have to ask to receive help from angels. You have to initiate the conversation to have a talk with angels. Once you have established your communication, you can receive more from them than you would by only asking when you are desperate for help. You do need to own your personal space even from angels. You are responsible for your thoughts, actions, and all of your creativity. Thus you need to create what is correct for you regardless of what any other being says.

Angels are a gift from God. They can help us with everything from our physical survival to our spiritual awakening and purpose. As the world vibration increases, our opportunities increase for spiritual communication. Everyone on Earth can learn to talk with angels. Interaction with angels can be an experience of wonder and joy.

Devils are another story. These are souls that are not in alignment with God. They are in competition with God instead of in agreement. Most everyone has a little of the devil in them. Very few souls on Earth are in complete agreement with God's will. Most souls have a level of competition with God in fighting for what they want instead of what God wants. We often act in a mean fashion rather than a kind one or are impatient instead of patient. We even escalate to greater extremes and choose greed over generosity and fear over love. We can clear the "devils" within by learning to let go and stop judging. We can replace fear with love and put ourselves back in alignment with God. We can remember our God-given role and respond to it with joy. By realigning with God and doing what we came to Earth to do, we clear the "devils" from our lives.

What we often call devils from outside ourselves are beings who took a body and became engulfed in the physical world. When they left the body, they were so caught on some aspect of the world that they chose to remain locked into it to be near their addiction instead of moving along their spiritual path. They did not align with the Cosmic Consciousness, but competed with it. This world is a seductive place and many souls become so involved with some aspect of it they do not want to free themselves to be spirit. They hold on to the physical world to be near whatever it is for which they have given up their freedom. They are caught within the Earth plane without a body through which to create. These are souls who chose not to clear their inner "devils" to align with God.

A soul can become addicted to anything on Earth; another person, a place, alcohol, tobacco, any drug, sex, an emotion such as hate, or any of the strong experiences of this world such as power. When a soul is addicted in life, he or she may stay that way after death. When you hear of someone having a haunted house, that is what has happened. A soul has gotten stuck on that place because of some powerful experience there. Anyone who is spiritually aware can help the soul regain its freedom and move on.

The souls caught on the Earth plane after the death of the body are often malevolent. They carry disturbing levels of emotion with them into the spiritual plane. They are not allowed to leave the Earth plane until they work out their problem. While they are focused on Earth, they are often trying to work their problems out through other souls in bodies. While there is spiritual help for these souls to overcome their problems, they often refuse assistance and spend their energy deviling others.

These beings will invade any other soul's body to experience their addiction. They will invade and abuse others to satisfy their desires. The soul whose body is used is responsible for whatever occurs, thus every soul must own his own body and avoid being invaded by the souls who are caught in the prison of physical beliefs.

A woman who had been abused by both of her parents had the opportunity to face her creations and overcome them. Instead, she chose to ignore her past and deny its effect on her. Her ego was more important to her than healing herself or loving others. She opened to the spiritual world without first cleansing her vessel, her body. She was invaded by a malevolent being very quickly and used to disrupt many lives. She was so invaded by the being that she refused help to remove it from her system. She eventually dropped away from the spiritual world and immersed herself completely in the physical world. She chose the physical and in the process lost a great deal.

The best way to avoid interaction with these earthbound souls is to heal yourself of anything they can use to enter your personal space. If you are addicted to cocaine, you are vulnerable to any soul that is stuck on that drug and is looking for a body through which to experience it. If you have sexual abuse pictures, you are not only vulnerable to your pictures but also to an earthbound soul that is seeking an avenue to experience its addiction in the physical world.

Personal healing through meditation can free you from the "devils" of this world whether they are another soul trying to use your space or your own pictures and concepts that cause you to misuse your energy. You have nothing to fear from these souls when you are in alignment with God. Only when you are not in alignment with God can these beings bother you. If you feel out of touch with God, you can always ask for help from an angel.

The fear of these earthbound beings is what gives them the greatest power. There is no need to be afraid of them as they do not have any power of their own. You give them any power they have by being afraid, resisting, or harboring the very thing to which they are addicted. You can overcome your fear, your resistance, and you can clear your disturbing experiences. One of the reasons angels are so numerous is that we need their help to safely steer through the temptations and dangers of the world of matter.

The easiest way to tell the difference between an angel and an earthbound soul is that you have to ask the angel for help and the earthbound soul will offer you all manner of "help" without your asking. The "devil" will offer you all you believe that you want if you let it use your body. The thing you may lose in the process is yourself. You as spirit may find that you become an earthbound soul also if you listen to the voice of these temptations. Like the slogan encouraging children to refuse drugs, "Just say no."

We must all be aware of our personal space and own it for our spiritual purpose. Whether we have to deal with outside "devils" or the "devils" we have created within ourselves, we can do this with our spiritual awareness and help from God. Everyone has one form of devil or another to overcome. No one is able to avoid this process of choice. Even Jesus had his time of trial or choice between the temptations of Earth and the freedom of spirit. Jesus owned his space and chose the spiritual path. He did this to remind us that even though it is not always easy, we can also choose the spiritual way to freedom.

The most important thing to remember when learning about and relating to any being without a physical body is that your body belongs to you and you alone. God is the most important focus for all of us and when you are tuned into God you can see clearly and be unafraid. Whether a being is offering assistance or interference, you and your relationship with God are of the utmost importance. God loves everything and everyone. God loves both the "angels" and "devils" of this world. We can learn to love both aspects of ourselves and gain greater freedom to develop love within. To God, there is no "good" or "bad" only love.

Love God and all of your interactions, communications, and creations will be what you need.

YOU AND YOUR LARGER BODY:
PLANET EARTH

We are spirit. Those who are reading this book have a physical body. We also have a collective physical body. The planet Earth is the body of our collective spiritual consciousness. We are all one in spirit and the body we are manifesting through is planet Earth. The Earth is an alive, growing thing just as our bodies are alive. We gain a new perspective of our planet when we see it as our alive larger body.

The Earth is like the Garden of Eden in the Judeo-Christian Bible story. We are the gardeners of Earth. Just as we as individuals are responsible for our body, we as a collective consciousness are responsible for our larger body, planet Earth. Unfortunately, we have not done a good job of tending our garden. We have destroyed a great deal of the natural beauty and productivity of the planet through greed, fear, doubt, and other misguided states of being. We forgot that we are spirit, that we are all connected, and that Earth is our creative paradise. Our paradise is now a mess in some places since we misused it or did not tend it properly.

You know that if you do not take care of your physical body, it will not function well and will eventually become ill. This is true of Earth also. If you do not give your body enough food, sleep, exercise or whatever it needs, your body will rebel. If you overindulge your body, it will react also. If you mistreat your body with various substances or keep it in a state of fear or hate, it will eventually have a physical reaction to get your attention to correct the situation. Our planet is like our body and is reacting to the ways we have mistreated it. The planned-for changes occurring on Earth are more difficult because of our mismanagement of our larger body. When we wake up to our spiritual nature and operate from this spiritual perspective, the transitions are easier. We know what to do and how to do it instead of blundering around in the darkness caused by physical blinders.

Many physical body illnesses are the result of mistreatment or misuse of the body. Many of the planetary disturbances we are experiencing are a result of our mistreatment of Earth. We take all of the trees, gold, oil or other gifts like greedy children who want more than their share. We do not tend the Earth like a garden but take from her as if we are thieves in the night. We need to remember that Earth is our creative space and when related to in a healthy manner, we can create an abundance and never lack for anything.

Instead, we often take away without replenishing and destroy without thought. We do not acknowledge that the depletion of trees is having an effect on the atmosphere and on erosion. Pollution of waterways and seas is affecting the food chain. Destruction of mountains for metals changes the watershed. Industrial pollution and exhaust from automobiles alter the air we breathe. Wars disrupt life and create famine. The list of our mismanagement is a long one and detailed in many places. Even the intellect can comprehend what we are doing, yet most people appear to be uninterested in changing our relationship with Earth. Power games, greed, and hate often prevail over common sense.

Earth is strong, filled with life and abundance, and continues to sustain us regardless of our foolishness. What paradise would we create if we related to Earth with a spiritual perspective? How many bodies would Earth nourish with proper care? We limit our sight with fear and expectations instead of looking at all we can do on this planet if we work as spirit. We can create a healthy relationship with Earth and have greater abundance than we can presently perceive if we remember we are spirit and the Earth is our larger body.

Most people do not even have a healthy relationship with their own body. This is the first step for many. Everyone needs to relate to his or her body in a responsible manner. When this personal responsibility

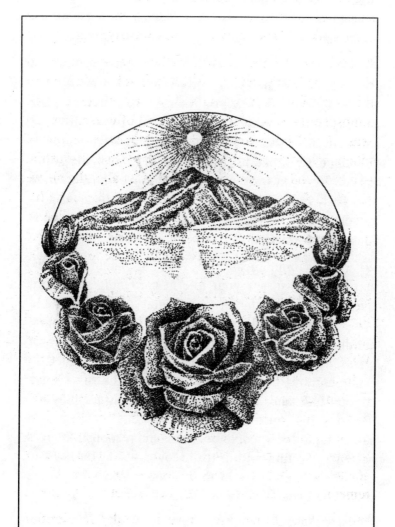

What paradise would we create if we related to Earth with a spiritual perspective?

is accomplished in personal space, it is easy for it to expand into the larger space of Earth. When you are taking care of your piece of our collective space, you are doing your most important part.

By recognizing that your body is your vessel or your temple for the lifetime, you realize that it is important to keep it in a state of health, both physically and spiritually. When you treat your body with respect, you can easily treat other bodies with respect, including Earth. You can turn within and discover how to treat your body by listening to it. You can also discover how to relate best to planet Earth by listening to your spiritual information and to the planet itself.

When you communicate with your body and the planet, you can learn to see your role in gardening the Earth. Everyone has a different part to play in caring for the planet. Some will do physical work, such as gardening, building, cleaning, transporting, caring for animals or plants, recycling, inventing or other things needed to create an abundant life for everyone on Earth. Others do spiritual and educational work such as praying, manipulating cosmic and earth energies, healing, and educating to help people be aware and responsible. It is necessary to turn within to discover what you need to do. There are many jobs to be done. When you do the work you need to do, you can do it with joy. You can learn to love what you are called to do instead of looking for the illusive perfect role or the one that brings only financial gain. Any work can be a joy when it is done with love.

First, you need to master your personal space or you may not understand how to deal with the larger space through your work or other creative endeavors. If you cannot function through your own body with spiritual seniority, you can be disturbing and even dangerous to yourself and others. If you decide to be a conservationist and do not understand yourself, you could be more harmful than helpful. Like the missionary who does not look within and understand her reasons for teaching her religious beliefs outside of her own realm of experience, you could disrupt rather than heal the environment. If you attempt to change through judgement and hate, you will add to the destruction. You need to learn to see things as they are, let go of judgement, and then allow the change. If you try to force people or the planet into your ideal mold, you will be like the missionary trying to change people into her perfect concept. You will be frustrated and disappointed, and the planet will be filled with that much more disruption.

The Earth is a living body just as your body is a living thing. You have within you the information you need about yourself as spirit and your physical body. You also have the intelligence to educate yourself about the physical world. The important thing is to realize that you are spirit and have a responsibility to your personal body and to the collective body of Earth. You can easily discover your role in the play of life by turning within to your spiritual information. You can use your spiritual abilities to learn what needs to be done and your intelligence to understand how to do your part.

Most groups that we call primitive have a working relationship with the Earth. They live with what is provided and create what they consider an abundance. Few of these groups believe in ownership of property. Most of them see the Earth as alive and like a mother provider to be treated with respect and reverence. These groups live in balance when they are not disturbed by industrial societies that destroy their environment. They create their life experience from a strong spiritual perspective.

Even in an industrial society you can change your relationship with your body and with the Earth. You can get to know your personal body and your larger body and relate to them both in a healing manner. If you do not have a healing relationship with your personal body, you need to start there. By healing your body, you heal the larger body. You have to clean up your small part before you can be effective in cleaning up larger portions of the planet. If you learn to talk to your body, you can eventually learn to talk to your larger body, the Earth.

Whenever you notice a flower, tree, rock, or any part of the Earth, you see an aspect of the body of Earth. In the same way, you pay attention to your own body by noticing any part or aspect of your body. You do not need to have a degree in anatomy to talk to or understand your body, nor do you need a global understanding to communicate with your bigger body, Earth. All you need for communication is a desire to do so and a belief that you can.

You will soon learn what your body and the body of Earth need from you. You will also discover what these bodies have to offer you. There is a possibility of joyous harmony that can be awakened through awareness and communication. Be still and listen. You may be amazed at what you hear. Learn to love your body and you can learn to love the Earth. The term "earthy" has many connotations. I like to think of "earthy" as rich, abundant, exciting, sensual and full of life. The dark soil being plowed, trees full of fruit, a lioness stalking her prey, a belly dancer exuding fertility, and children playing all display the wealthy, joyous qualities of Earth. The endless possibilities for joy and experience on this planet are amazing. Even experiences of loss and grief give us opportunities for growth.

When you accept your body as a body with its aspects of time, space, mass, gravity, birth, death, effort and many other qualities, you have the ingredients for a life of learning with joy. The great teachers all accepted their bodies and used them fully. Jesus' first miracle was turning water into wine at a wedding. This event and its symbolism tell us to use everything God has given us to unite with God and to enjoy the earthly part of the process. When we accept the body as it is, we can more easily acknowledge ourselves as spirit without time, space, mass, effort, or any earthly limits.

The Earth is a rich environment for us to use to create within and through. The Earth can be a healing place for growth and change. It is filled with opportunities for us to learn and grow. Whether we are healing our personal body of some imbalance or assisting to heal the larger body of Earth of an imbalance, we can use the vibrations of Earth to help the healing process. We can spiritually pull energies from the Earth to change vibrations. We can use our bodies as the creative communication vehicles they are meant to be. We can be still and listen to the Earth and all of its inhabitants to learn about ourselves, the Earth and God.

We grow and change as spirit, our bodies grow and change, and our larger body Earth also grows and changes. Accepting our growth as a natural phenomenon can help the flow and make our healing process light and joyous. Every time we change as spirit, our body has to make a corresponding change. As more spiritual energy pours into the Earth, this larger body has to make changes and adjustments also. Physical growth comes from spiritual change, and we have to remember that physical bodies respond differently than spirit. Clear sight and wise management of our personal bodies and our larger body can make the present dramatic growth time much easier. We also need to remember that we are spirit and not our body or our larger body, Earth. We are not bound by the physical limits of the physical world and can learn to bring our spiritual abilities and qualities to play in the physical scene. When we remember that we are immortal and part of God, we can remain neutral and compassionate as drastic changes occur.

The slogans to save the whales and the dolphins have always amazed me. The dolphins and whales are the ones who need to save us as they are more awake than many humans. They are finally making contact with us in Mexico, England, and other parts of the globe, as we release our fears and slow down enough to listen to them. We need to listen to their song of harmony. We need to listen to the planet and our sisters and brothers who share it so we can again create as the gardeners we were originally meant to be. Our planet has a song and everything on it sings. Many have become deaf to the music of others and have forgotten to play their intended part. We need to remember how to sing our song.

Now is the time to awaken to the music of Earth and the song of every living thing on and in the Earth. If we listen and hear the song, we will want to join in the harmony. If we insist on screaming out our personal desires and demands, whether they are personal or appear universal, we will not hear the love song of Earth. When we hear this song of love, we can answer it with our note of love and the entire environment, which we are cooperatively creating, will be enhanced.

EARTH CHANGES

This period of time on Earth is a planned-for aspect of spiritual evolution. Everything on Earth is coming of age including the planet. We are experiencing the inflow of God's energy and the impact on all physical as well as spiritual phenomena. As the Earth and all it contains increases in vibration and balances its energy, everything changes with it. The experience on Earth at this time is one of drastic change and healing. We need to be in touch with ourselves as spirit and with God to achieve what we are meant to do during this time. We have made this spiritual and physical transition much more difficult than it needs to be by not being in touch with God. We can lessen the destruction and enhance our journey by returning our attention to God now.

The body Earth is going through a major transition.

The Earth is cleansing energy that is destructive to it and bringing in spiritual energy to heal itself. If we look at the Earth as our larger body, we can see that it is going through a giant growth period just as we go through growth in our individual bodies. This time of growth is more dramatic because we have not treated our larger body as a temple but like a garbage dump. We have not been loving, gentle caretakers but have been abusive and hateful to our larger body. The Earth is having to cleanse itself of the abuse we have heaped upon it. This is not the first time we have experienced such a change, and it will not be the last. While the increase in energy and the vast changes are part of our original plan, the amount of disturbance and destruction is caused by our separation from God and the resulting mismanagement of our physical world.

There are many books being written about what will happen physically on Earth in the next few years. Many people are getting messages through their dreams. Other people are hearing voices about the coming events while still others are seeing visions and knowing new information. It is time for us to talk openly about the changes that are coming and work together to retain the development we wish to keep. Spiritual work is needed as well as physical work. The difficult task is balancing spiritual and physical needs during times of confusion, since the physical pull is so strong. By preparing on both levels now, we can work more effectively during times of stress.

Most people want to focus on the physical, but the most important issue is spiritual work. Every soul on planet

Earth needs to realign with God. This realignment will not only accomplish what we are here to do as individuals but will also lessen the destruction that will occur without our communication with God. Every soul is meant to relate directly with God, without clergy or church in between. Every soul is a part of God and needs this communication to fulfill his or her life purpose. We need to experience the love from God to give us the strength to choose to return that love. It is not necessary to know the future to do the correct thing. Through communication with God, one can know the correct action every moment. God gives what we need if we listen.

Regardless of what happens to your individual body or the collective body of Earth, the most important thing is to communicate with God. Those who choose to relate to God will be given opportunities to keep their present body to continue their growth into the next era. If they lose their body during the changes, they will be allowed to return to participate in the exciting growth opportunity available during the coming spiritually focused time or they will return to a union with God. The souls who choose to stay focused on physical things such as money, judgement, sex, righteousness, drugs, physical power, competition with God, and so forth will not be able to function in the new energy level. These souls will be given the opportunity to continue their growth in other times and environments. Alignment with God is essential for a transition into the new level of awareness and energy on planet Earth.

Our growth as a collective consciousness is taking us

into more group interaction. We are learning how to function in groups and retain our individual nature. Groups have always been important for survival, communication, and creativity. Groups are especially important now because of the physical demands brought on by the changes in each individual and in the Earth, as well as the need for each individual to mature into a state of communion and interaction. A group can provide safety and support that cannot be created individually and can provide a wealth of skills and communication. Groups need some form of structure to create order and at the same time enough flexibility to allow for individual purpose. The group must never override the relationship of the individual soul with God.

There are leaders and teachers available for you to follow and groups for you to join. You need to learn to have your personal connection with God whether you relate to a group or not. If you choose to work with a group at this time, be sure the emphasis is on the individual's relationship with God. If the emphasis is on the teacher, leader, or group, that is not a safe group. You must worship only God. Do not allow yourself to be involved in worshipping a leader or group. Use the group, but do not lose yourself in it.

The Earth will change in ways that we cannot at this time comprehend. We will need to shift our perspective of reality drastically. The way to do this is to develop a spiritual perspective. When we relate to God, we can deal with the physical changes. Without the connection with God and God's messengers, we will be lost in fear and insanity because of the vastness of the changes. The human body and brain cannot operate rapidly enough to deal with the coming transition without spiritual guidance. We must rely on ourselves as spirit, God, and the spiritual realm to get through this time.

This time of change is one of great celebration. When we see the spiritual perspective of it, we can rejoice. Everyone is being given the opportunity to cleanse past evil from their individual bodies, and our larger body, the Earth, is cleansing evil also. This will allow everyone who chooses to operate in a spiritual fashion as more spiritual energy and awareness flow into the planet. We can enjoy the Earth's growth when we have a spiritual view. Many will believe they are in hell if they maintain a physical view. As spirit, we can see that everyone and everything is meant to grow into a new level of spiritual functioning and awareness.

This time of change is similar to puberty for the body. It is a time of excitement and fear, of high energy and adventure, of new horizons and letting go of childhood and the past. It is a time of imploding and exploding where everything appears new and unfamiliar. As a species we are moving from childhood into adulthood with all of the accompanying rewards and challenges. It is our choice whether to move into adulthood with difficulty or with grace.

You can begin now to clear your body for your personal changes and help the world experience joy in this transition. You can make your life easier, and you can then assist others who have not done the cleansing when things speed up. As more energy enters this area of space, the vibration increases and moves deeper into matter. The more engulfed in matter the soul is, the longer it takes energy to reach them. You can either wait until the vibration is high enough to awaken you, or you can wake up now and cleanse and prepare to help others. You do not have to wait until the higher vibration shakes you awake. You can wake up now and get started. Your meditation and communication with God will help you clear your body so you can be in touch with your spiritual self and enter this awakened state. You can direct your physical reality from your spiritual perspective. You can learn to see what is happening and can make clear, responsible decisions about your life.

Two things we must clear from ourselves are fear and doubt since these vibrations disrupt our connection with God. We need to clear these disrupters and create love, faith and certainty to have our spiritual view. We need to have faith in God and certainty about our ability to fulfill our purpose and return God's love. Every soul has a purpose and every soul has a direct connection with God to assist him to fulfill that purpose. God is always present. We simply need to return our attention to God.

The changes that take place on the planet will be reflected within each individual body. There will be times of immense personal disturbance for most people. Many will believe they have lost their "sanity." Everyone will be clearing fear, hate, greed, doubt, pain, competition or whatever they have stored within the body. We will be gaining seniority with and clearing not only our own energies but any of these energies that we accepted from others as well.

After a soul has completed the most intense part of cleansing, they are able to enjoy and use the higher vibrations available. This spiritually awakened state can be a joyous experience where one is spiritually in charge of physical creativity. It is well worth doing the work to have this level of spiritual creativity. The present moment is where we can experience this transition so do not worry about the past or future. Respond to what is happening now, and awakening can be exciting. The world is changing, bodies are changing, everyone and everything is changing. Let go and enjoy!

SPIRITUAL TECHNIQUES

During this time of vast change and spiritual awakening, we need to have a spiritual focus. Spiritual techniques help us create and maintain this focus. When we focus spiritually, we are able to stay in touch with ourselves as spirit, with our bodies, with the planet, and with God. By using spiritual techniques, we train our bodies to accept us as spirit and to accept the increased energy that is coming into the planet.

We have all used physical techniques such as exercise programs, diets, therapy and so forth to create our life. It is time to use spiritual techniques to create in order to manifest on the level of higher energy that is now available. By operating as spirit through spiritual concepts, we move to a new stage in our development. We move from being engulfed in and manipulated by matter to being in charge of the matter we have created.

You can begin to have a more spiritually focused life by creating as spirit rather than allowing your body to create through its desires. Instead of reacting emotionally to every situation, you can learn to use spiritual techniques such as grounding and centering in neutral to respond rather than react to a situation. You can re-train your body to allow you to be in charge instead of the body running the show.

Bodies are very capable, powerful, and seductive. Spirit is capable and powerful beyond the body's comprehension. It is simply a matter of training the body to accept spirit and reminding spirit how to create through a body. You may want to think of using your body like training a beautiful and spirited horse. You want the horse to retain its spirit and vitality and also respond to your wishes. As spirit, you want your body to create your desires and not its wishes while retaining the body's vitality. By loving the body and creating through it with awareness and care, you can create a harmonious relationship.

Spiritual techniques help us accomplish this training process. By grounding ourselves as spirit through the body into this reality, we can relate to the present scene and the specific body and circumstances. All the techniques help spirit remember how to manipulate physical energy and help the body raise its energy to accept spirit. As spirit and body begin to harmonize, communication increases and the techniques become habits like walking and talking.

When you internalize the techniques as part of your daily life, you begin to live your meditation. You are able to be in tune with yourself as spirit and with your body. You can see and know what is you and what is your body as well as what belongs to someone else. Life takes on new meaning when you have this spiritual view instead of the confused one where you believe that you are your body and the energy you stored in it.

By using spiritual techniques to train yourself, you realize that you are spirit and not your body or your creations. You are not your job, your children, your spouse, or any of your creations; you are spirit. Through your spiritual training, you can move to a state above the physical pull to view your creations and experience a new relationship with them. You can find a new level of love for all that you know when you are not engulfed by it all.

Most importantly, the techniques can lead you to your one-to-one communication with God. This personal connection that you are meant to have with God will open all of the doors of the Cosmos for you. Through the inner gate, you will discover God and through God you will find all things. By finding God within, you will know your true self, and all of life will be clearer to you.

The techniques presented here are grounding, centering in your head, creating and destroying the mental image picture of a rose, running earth and cosmic energy, being in present time, understanding the aura as your personal space, and deprogramming. All these techniques except deprogramming are taught in greater detail in the Key Series[4] of spiritual textbooks.

Meditation is necessary to attain an inner focus and a listening relationship with God. The techniques described here and in the Key Series can help you quiet your body system and increase your spiritual awareness. The techniques can also help you raise the vibration of your body so you can move more freely into and through the body.

These techniques are meant to be used in daily life as well as in your quiet meditation times. You can be grounded while meditating or while eating dinner with your family. You can use most of the techniques at any time. Practice will help you use the techniques automatically so that when the dinner scene becomes rowdy you can ground, center, and respond instead of getting angry and reacting.

Avoid getting serious or using effort when practicing spiritual techniques as these body energies will stop the flow of energy. When I get serious about the techniques, I remember a story about a friend who is a black belt in karate. He is an expert in this discipline. One night while walking through a dark area in San Francisco, he was attacked by a thief. Instead of remembering all of his karate training, he jumped on the guy and bit his ear. The thief was frightened away, and my friend was not hurt. He laughed all the way home at his instant body reaction. His training helped him overcome his fear and be able to protect himself when threatened even if the details of karate had eluded him for the moment.

Learn the techniques and the purpose of them will become a part of your life even if you do not remember to do them perfectly all the time. If you ground regularly, you will be grounded when you need to be. If you forget your grounding, instead of judging yourself, laugh and go on to learn the lesson provided. My friend learned that he did not have to be a perfect karate expert to protect himself, and you can learn that you can operate as spirit without becoming a perfect meditator. Remember that only God is perfect, and you will be relieved of a great many expectations of yourself.

Learning is always easier when you have fun. Enjoy your practice with the techniques whether you are using them to meditate quietly by yourself or using them to maneuver your way through daily life. Acknowledge the times you operate as spirit, and you will learn when it is easy and when you need to pay attention. Keeping a journal can help you enjoy your learning process and validate your progress.

To learn the techniques, sit on a straight-backed chair in a quiet place. Be alone to experience your unique energy without distractions. Put your feet flat on the floor and your hands separated in your lap. Sit as straight as possible as your spine is a channel for your energy. Close your eyes and turn within when you practice each technique.

Have fun getting to know yourself as spirit and re-acquainting yourself with God.

GROUNDING

Everything is energy. Every cell in your body has an electrical charge. Your system is energy, and like all energy, it is safer if you ground it. By grounding, you connect your electrical energy to the energy of your body and the energy of your body to the energy of the planet. This connectedness allows for a flow of energy, communication, and a new level of control.

When you are in control, the system is safer. You can manipulate your energy easily and create what you want. If you are not grounded, you feel out of touch with physical reality, are easily frightened, and often feel disturbed. A body without grounding is similar to a boat without a keel, a house without a lightening rod, or a kite without a string.

Grounding provides a foundation, connection, and release system for all of your energies. You can let energy flow down your grounding cord to the center of the Earth to release it from your system as well as using your grounding as a connection to the physical world.

An energy center containing your information about this world and how to function within it is located near the base of your spine. Your grounding cord flows from this energy center to the center of the Earth to create a connection between you and your physical creations.

TO GROUND sit in a chair, close your eyes, and visualize a flow of energy from the energy center near the base of your spine to the center of the Earth.

WITH YOUR EYES CLOSED and your body sitting quietly, experience your grounding cord. Notice how it affects your body. Are you relaxed, tense, or in transition? Use your grounding to get to know your body and your relationship with it.

TAKE A FEW DEEP BREATHS and let the energy flow down your grounding cord, from your body to the center of the Earth. Create your connection with the Earth and take charge of your creativity.

SIT QUIETLY and experience your grounding cord.

TO INCREASE YOUR GROUNDING let more energy flow down your grounding cord. Own your grounding cord as your creation and increase the flow of energy down it at any time. The more energy you bring into your body, the more you need to increase your grounding.

USE YOUR GROUNDING to release energy. Visualize tension from your body flowing down your grounding cord to the center of the Earth.

YOU CAN RELEASE anything from your body or energy system down your grounding cord. Release emotional energy down your grounding cord, such as anger, that you are having difficulty controlling.

GROUND and be aware of yourself as spirit creating through your body. Be aware of your connection to the Earth as your larger creative space.

Practice using your grounding cord in a variety of circumstances. Use it while meditating, at work, while relating to your family, or any time you remember to use it. The more you consciously ground, the better you are able to ground.

Grounding gives you spiritual control in the physical world.

CENTERING IN YOUR HEAD

You are spirit, not your body. You appear as a bright light. You can be any place at any time, but your body has to travel through time and space. You are able to control your physical creativity best from the space in the center of your head. This space is your control tower. You as spirit have many resources for communicating, controlling, and creating located in this space in your head.

The center of your head contains your information about neutrality and spiritual sight. You are able to see your world from a neutral, clear perspective when you look from your head. The physical and the spiritual eyes are located in your head so this is the place to be in order to see on both levels.

You need to be aware of what is happening for you as spirit as well as what is occurring for the body to maintain a safe environment. If you focus your attention into other areas of your body, you will be overwhelmed by that aspect of the system. If you focus in the abdominal area of the body, you will have your attention on your survival, sexual, and emotional energies. This is a limited view of your total creativity.

The center of your head gives you the full view of your physical world without overwhelming you with the physical senses and desires of the body. It allows you as spirit to be in the body without becoming the body. The body is such a strong force you need to learn how to create through it without losing yourself in the physical scene.

The center of your head also gives you a neutral view so you can see your creations without judging them. This allows you to change things without wasting time with judgement. You can also learn to accept yourself and others as you and they are, instead of trying to change everything all the time.

While it is helpful to leave your body at times, such as when you sleep and at times during meditation, your clearest way of relating to the body is from the center of your head.

TO BE IN THE CENTER OF YOUR HEAD, ground and focus your attention into your head a little above and behind your eyes. Experience being at your pineal gland or in front of it.

YOU ARE SPIRIT and can be anyplace. Put your attention in your head and you will go there.

SIT QUIETLY in an upright position, feet on the floor and hands separate. Be grounded and in the center of your head. Notice how your body reacts to you being in your head.

MOVE ABOVE YOUR HEAD about a foot and experience being outside of your body. Move back into the center of your head and notice the difference. Practice moving above your body and back into your head to become confident about being in your head.

BE IN THE CENTER OF YOUR HEAD and experience your body around you. You are light and the body is heavy. You do not have effort, but the body uses effort for every movement. Feel, see, and experience the differences.

You are able to function more fully as spirit in the physical world when you operate from the center of your head. You can see yourself and others as spirit and see the differences between you and your body. You can see that all creations are ultimately spiritual ones, and life on Earth is an opportunity to learn as spirit.

CREATING AND DESTROYING ON EARTH

Earth is a place of constant change. The process of creation includes destruction. The seasons demonstrate the creation-destruction cycle on Earth. A volcano is a good example of this process as in its destructive explosion it creates new soil, weather changes, and a variety of landscape alterations.

As spirit, we create and destroy to maintain a healing balance in our lives. We create adulthood and destroy childhood. We create marriage and destroy a state of being single. We destroy a tree and use it to build a house. We are always in motion and this motion involves constant change.

We can take charge of our creative process as spirit by being conscious of what we create and destroy. We are ideally meant to know what we are creating in our lives so we can make aware, intelligent decisions about our path through life. We are mature when we create consciously and immature when we create without awareness.

The symbol of a rose can be used to help you create consciously. The rose, like the lotus, represents the unfolding of spirit to God. By using a symbol, you avoid the emotionality associated with most of your creations.

TO CREATE CONSCIOUSLY, ground and be in the center of your head. Take a few deep breaths to relax your body and release unwanted energy down your grounding cord.

FROM THE CENTER OF YOUR HEAD, create the mental image picture of a rose six to eight inches in front of your forehead.

DESTROY THE ROSE. Let it disappear, explode or melt away.

CREATE ANOTHER ROSE and destroy it. Practice creating and destroying roses until you are comfortable with the technique.

CREATE A ROSE representing something you want to release and destroy the rose. Repeat creating and destroying the rose symbol until you have released the unwanted energy.

You can create and destroy roses to clear your head or any other part of your space. You cleanse your system by creating and destroying roses. You can do this at any time or place to help you be clear and to take charge of your body and space.

If you are out of control with an emotion such as anger or grief, you can ground and create and destroy roses to regain control of your body and its emotions. You will eventually be able to move back into your head and regain spiritual control. The more you practice this technique in your meditations, the more you will be able to use it in your daily life on an automatic basis.

We are constantly creating and destroying whether we are conscious of this process or not. By learning to be conscious of our creative process, we take control of it and learn to be responsible for our creations. Whether we use the technique to clear our space during meditation, or gain control of our emotions during an argument, we are operating consciously as spirit.

EARTH AND COSMIC ENERGY

We are spirit and create through our bodies. We need the energy of both the Earth and the Cosmos to accomplish this level of creativity. Earth and cosmic energies are available to us in unlimited varieties and amounts. We can use both energies to balance our spirit-body dichotomy. This balance allows us to change and grow, to heal, to learn our lessons and to maintain spiritual consciousness without losing awareness of our body and physical reality.

Earth energy is the vibrations of the Earth, and cosmic energy is the vibrations of the Cosmos. Earth energy is slower than cosmic energy. Both energies are necessary for life on Earth. We need to remember how to use both in a balanced fashion to create consciously.

The meditation technique of running earth and cosmic energies allows you to consciously control your energy flow and focus. Everyone and everything is already energy in motion. By manipulating your energy in a particular fashion, you take control of the pattern and focus the energy as you wish it to be. Here on planet Earth we are meant to create, and these energies can help you focus your attention to create consciously.

GROUND, be in the center of your head, and create and destroy a rose. Sit up as straight as possible with your feet on the floor, your hands and feet separate and your spine straight. Breathe deeply and relax.

BE AWARE of your feet. There are energy centers in the arches of your feet. Allow earth energy to flow up through the centers at the arches of your feet and move up through channels in your legs to the energy center near the base of your spine. Let the energy flow down your grounding cord to the center of the Earth.

BE STILL and experience earth energy moving up your leg channels to the energy center near the base of your spine and flowing down your grounding cord. Allow the earth energy to melt away any blocks to the flow of this energy.

LET EARTH ENERGY help you be in touch with the planet Earth. Feel the connection you have with Earth through your grounding and earth energy. Let the earth energy flow up through your legs and down your grounding, helping you to be more attached to the Earth.

FOCUS IN THE CENTER OF YOUR HEAD. Create and destroy a rose to clear your space. Be aware of the top of your head.

BRING COSMIC ENERGY into the top of your head, slightly to the back of your head, and let it flow down channels on each side of your spine to the energy center near the base of your spine.

MIX THE COSMIC AND EARTH ENERGIES and let them flow up through channels running through the front of your body to the top of your head. Allow the energy to fountain out the top of your head and flow all around your body. Let some of the energy move through channels in your shoulders and arms out the palms of your hands.

BE STILL AND ENJOY the flow of energy through your system. Let the earth energy flow up your leg channels and down your grounding cord and the cosmic energy flow down your back channels and up your front channels and out your arm channels.

LET ENERGY FLOW freely all around you. Be in the center of your head and grounded and be aware of consciously running your energy. Allow time to run these energies.

Running earth and cosmic energies is a cleansing and balancing process. You create change by cleansing your system. You create healing by continuing to run your energies and balancing the new space you create by cleansing.

You will begin to experience a new spiritual awareness as you continue to run your energies during your meditations. If you practice, you can learn to run your energies in this conscious fashion most of the time.

In this way, you are constantly cleansing your system. Since you are always picking up energy and concepts from outside of yourself, this is helpful for you to separate what you want to keep and what you want to release.

You can be grounded, in the center of your head, and running earth and cosmic energies any time. You will benefit from this process most if you allow a minimum of thirty minutes of quiet time to do this each day. You will eventually learn the techniques enough to take them into your daily life.

REVIEW THE PROCESS by grounding, being in the center of your head and creating and destroying a rose. From the center of your head, move earth energy up your leg channels and down your grounding. Move your cosmic energy down each side of your spine, mix in some earth energy, and move it up the channels in the front of your body. Let the energy fountain out the top of your head and flow around your body. Allow some of the energy to flow down your arms and out your hands.

BE QUIET and enjoy the flow of energy through your system. Let any unwanted energy flow down your grounding cord and create and destroy a rose to release energy.

These techniques are for preparing yourself to communicate and operate as spirit and can lead you into a quiet space of meditation or help you move through your daily life with a spiritual perspective. Whether you are quietly turning within or driving down a busy street, you can learn to operate as spirit through your body. Practice and you will reap the benefits.

YOUR AURA

Your aura is your personal space. It is the display of your energy in the physical world. Your aura is ideally a variety of vibrations which can be translated into color. There are usually a minimum of five vibrations clearly discernible in an aura. The most common number of layers in the aura is seven. There can be many more vibrations displayed depending on the development of the soul. The aura ideally goes all around your body, above your head, under your feet, and equally in back and front.

The aura is meant to be close around the physical body as an extension of the body space. A comfortable range can vary from six to twelve inches depending on the circumstances. The aura can be expanded to encompass the universe or contracted to the body itself. Neither of these extreme states of being are comfortable or practical.

Your aura as your personal space gives you a creative playground within which to create, communicate, and learn. You have been given this space by God and have the right to this space without interference from others. You have the freedom to create within your space.

The easiest way to own this space for yourself is to allow others to have their space. This means that you create within your aura and not outside of it. This can be a challenge as most people are taught to create outside of their space, to relate more to others than to themselves and even to be guilty or ashamed about focusing on self. Creating within your aura is a process of unlearning old habits and creating new ways of operating in the world.

Once a child can feed, clothe, and care for herself, the mother no longer needs to be within the child's personal space. Unfortunately, most people do not know this. The responsibility of the parent is to care for, teach, and protect the body, not to control the spiritual space. The soul that has that body is responsible for her space and what she creates within and through it.

Your aura is an area you need to know so you can learn about your personal space and how to own it and create through it. You are most effective as a creator when you create through your vibration and space.

GROUND your body to the center of the Earth. Focus yourself into the center of your head. Create a rose and release it and repeat creating and releasing roses for a moment.

BE AWARE of being inside your body, in the center of your head. Be aware of your aura around you. Notice how far down your body your aura comes.

CREATE AND DESTROY ROSES to help you bring your aura all around your body. Take a few deep breaths to help you expand or contract your aura to between six to twelve inches around your body.

BE STILL and feel your aura around your body. From the center of your head, be aware of your creative space.

RELEASE any unwanted energy or foreign vibrations

down your grounding cord and own your aura for yourself.

The process of becoming aware of and owning your aura takes time. Everything in the physical world takes time, so allow yourself time to learn and practice the techniques. You may practice the techniques for months before you get your aura all around you or close to your body, or you may experience this immediately. Be where you are and see yourself as you are, and your growth process will flow. Do not try to be something you are not, and your aura will shine with your light and your creativity.

Be yourself as spirit and you will be enlightened.

PRESENT TIME

The Earth and everything on it operates in time and through space. Your body is in present time. The planet Earth is in present time. God is in present time. We have created the illusion of past and future to give us the opportunity to learn major creative lessons without having to live with the results forever. Time and space are part of our creative lessons and benefits.

Without the illusion of time, your every thought would manifest as soon as you had thought it. This should make you ecstatic that you have past and future, since most people have some thoughts they would rather not have known much less physically manifested.

Present time is simply here and now, this moment. It is so simple that you may miss the point looking for something more complicated. You can experience it by focusing your attention on whatever you are doing at the moment. Your body is your best avenue into present time.

GROUND and be in the center of your head. Create and destroy roses to bring your attention to yourself and clear your space.

TUNE INTO YOUR BODY and listen to your heart beat. Listen to your breathing. Let your body draw you into the present. Pay attention to your body rhythms and let them bring your attention to the present moment.

USE YOUR GROUNDING to release the past and

future issues with which you are concerned.

BE STILL and be in the present. Listen to the Earth and Earth sounds to help you bring your attention into the present.

We can most easily relate to our earthly creations and our relationship with God when we are in the present. If we are focused on the past or future, these communications will be disrupted as Earth and God are in the present.

You can learn to use time for your lessons without losing the power of a present-time focus. Patience brings the future you have created, and forgiveness allows you to release the past. Be in the present when you meditate, and you will learn to be in the present in all areas of your life.

DEPROGRAMMING

Your body is similar to a computer. It is programmed to function in a particular manner. You as spirit, your parents, your educational system, your religion and all of your experiences on Earth are part of your body's programming. Your body is also programmed with information you have brought into it from your past lives. Your body is essentially a composite of the mental image pictures, symbols, and concepts which you have created and gathered during your existence as spirit.

Some of your programming - how to keep your body alive, for example - is valuable. Other programming is detrimental to your creative process. Your body is programmed to function in a particular way. If you do not like your behavior, you can deprogram your physical system and reprogram it just as you would a computer. You take away what you do not like and insert what you want.

The term, "deprogramming," has received some unpleasant publicity as if it were hocus pocus or something to fear. You program and deprogram yourself all through life. You also allow others to do the same. You can learn to take conscious control of this process of programming, deprogramming and reprogramming. You can clear anything you do not want, whether it is something you adopted from others, or something you created that you no longer need. This process is also called healing.

To function freely on Earth, we need to know how to create and destroy as spirit within our body. Programming and deprogramming are ways to do this. We can do this easily through meditation using the spiritual techniques. We also have time and space as a buffer zone to allow for change in case we decide we do not like the new program.

GROUND, be in the center of your head, and create and destroy roses for a moment to clear your system.

RUN YOUR EARTH AND COSMIC ENERGIES. Move earth energy up through your leg channels and down your grounding cord. Move cosmic energy down your back channels, up your front channels out the top of your head, and all around you through your aura. Allow some of the energy to flow down your arms and out your hands. Refer to the section[5] on this to refresh your memory.

GET IN TOUCH with one concept you have that you do not like. For example, the concept that you have to relate to your body through pain.

LET YOUR earth and cosmic energies flow to cleanse the system as you clear the concept. Create a rose for this idea and destroy it, repeating the process until you are aware of the idea melting away. Allow time for this clearing process.

SEND THE CONCEPT down your grounding cord. Let it go.

FROM THE CENTER of your head, fill the new space within you with your own vibration.

CONTINUE TO RUN YOUR ENERGIES and allow your system to adjust to the new space you created by clearing the old concept. Create and destroy roses to help you continue to clear associated concepts.

Deprogramming and reprogramming your system is as simple as using the techniques. You focus on a concept or mental image picture that you want to clear, use the techniques to clear it, and then fill your new space with your own neutral energy to complete the process. You may have to repeat this process several times or for a long period of time if you have a great deal of emotional energy invested in the concept. You can move through some issues quickly while others take time and patience.

You can learn to take charge of what you store within your body and what you create through by consciously cleansing your system and adding clear light. You can clean up your part of the world and create a loving space on planet Earth within your personal system.

You have the power and the knowledge to change the world by healing yourself. Most people only lack the faith to do it. If you spend a short time each day to focus on you and your body, you will experience results in a short time as you will begin to see the world in a different way. The world will be affected even if you do not see any physical results.

Everything is connected, so when you deprogram hate from your system, you have removed hate from the world. When you run energy, you bring cosmic and earth energies into the consciousness of the world. By grounding, you affect everything within and around you. You are your doorway to everything.

You will discover your path and goals by clearing the things that interfere with your clear view. Start with simple issues and work into more emotional issues so you can build your confidence in the techniques before getting involved in difficult changes. As you unfold to yourself, the world will unfold to you.

TALKING TO GOD, TALKING TO EARTH

You can talk directly with God. You can also talk directly with Earth. You are spirit and a part of God, and you have a body which is part of the Earth. You are like a cell of God and your body is like a cell of the Earth. You are ideally meant to be in touch with both God and the Earth. You need to learn to meditate and turn within to open the door to both of these natural communications. The way to everything is within you.

Most of industrial society has given up its spiritual communication. The intellectual focus has substituted physical things such as drugs, therapy, movies, television, sexual obsession and the many other stimulations and ways of avoiding ourselves as spirit and our creations. Most people want to blame the world's problems on someone else instead of looking within to see what can be cleared and balanced in themselves. Most of the world has forgotten that we are spirit and part of God, that we have responsibility for our bodies and our relationship with Earth. It is time for us to awaken to our spiritual nature.

Communicating with God is necessary to accomplish what we came here to do. Communicating with Earth is also necessary to accomplish what we came here to do. We have the talking part well rehearsed. We need to practice the listening part of communication. Meditation is the easiest way to be still and listen. We can learn to quiet our mind-body system and listen to God and to Earth. We soon discover that both sources have similar information from different view points:

one spiritual and one physical.

You will find it helpful to learn to communicate with yourself and your body first to help you take the step to communicating with God and the planet. You need to know what is happening within you so you will know if you are hearing God. Until you know yourself, you will have difficulty knowing anything else.

Everyone is able to talk with God. Relax and enjoy the communication.

GROUND, be in the center of your head, create and destroy roses to clear your space. Take a few deep breaths to relax your body.

RUN YOUR EARTH AND COSMIC ENERGIES to prepare your system for meditation and communication.

BE STILL in the center of your head and listen to your body. Allow it to tell you its emotions and needs. They may be simple or complex, just listen. Let yourself respond to your body.

BEGIN A DIALOGUE with your body to get to know it. Learn what you have stored in your body that you want to clear and begin changing your system. Listen to your body as you do this, as your body will need more time than you do for changes.

KNOW YOURSELF by tuning into you as spirit. Be aware of you, the bright spark of light in the center of your head. Know your beauty.

You may want to stay with the above exercise for some time before moving on to the next step, or you may wish to start this level of communication now. You know yourself and what is correct for you.

BE GROUNDED AND CENTERED with your energies running and be still.

SAY HELLO TO PLANET EARTH and let yourself be still and receive a response. It will vary according to your beliefs. You may hear a voice, see images, have feelings depending on your way of communicating.

ENJOY YOUR CONVERSATION for as long as you want. Do not limit your communication with expectations, guilt or other barriers.

CREATE AND DESTROY ROSES to clear your space after you have finished your interaction. You need to maintain your personal space with everyone and everything in order to sing your note.

BE STILL and in a meditative space with your energy running, your grounding connected, and you in the center of your head.

SAY HELLO TO GOD and receive a hello in return. Know that you are worthy of God's attention. Take time to communicate with God in your own way. You may hear a voice, see pictures or images, feel emotions, or silently know or experience this communication in any number of ways. It could sound like your own voice. Allow your communication with God to be as it is in the present for you.

BE STILL AND ENJOY YOUR TIME WITH GOD.

BRING YOUR ATTENTION BACK to the physical world. Check your grounding and energy flow and be in the center of your head. Create and destroy roses to clear your space of anything you stimulated during your spiritual communication.

You can communicate with God or the Earth at any time or place. You may want to communicate by asking God's blessing on your meditation, or asking the Earth for abundance with your life. You can talk to God as you drive to work and seek guidance and energy for creating a healing day. You can commune with the Earth any time you take a walk or see the sky or look out of a window. You can be in touch with the Earth if you are surrounded by city concrete even though it may not be as pleasant as being directly in contact with the Earth.

You are spirit and naturally in touch with God. You have a body which is naturally in touch with the Earth. You only need to recognize these things and your communication can flow easily and naturally. The Earth is your cathedral. Your body is your temple. You are meant to be in harmony with all things. Talk with God and you will find your way to harmonize. Talk with the Earth and you will learn that everything you need is provided. You are not alone. Listen and you will discover what a wealth of information and an abundance of sustenance is available for you.

Wake up to the reality that you are spirit and you have everything you need to accomplish your goals in the frontier of planet Earth. Your body is your creative expression. Are you loving it? The Earth can be your paradise. Are you taking care of it? God is with you. Are you with God?

You are the one who makes it happen. Begin now to create as spirit in the frontier of Earth.

NOTES

[1] For more information on chakras refer to CHAKRAS: *Key to Spiritual Opening* by Mary Ellen Flora

[2] The *Key Series* by Mary Ellen Flora is as follows:

MEDITATION: *Key to Spiritual Awakening*
HEALING: *Key to Spiritual Balance*
CLAIRVOYANCE: *Key to Spiritual Perspective*
CHAKRAS: *Key to Spiritual Opening*

[3] See note 1

[4] See note 2

[5] Chapter 11, SPIRITUAL TECHNIQUES - Earth and Cosmic Energy page 177

INDEX

abdomen, 171
abundance, 9, 18, 114, 148,
   150, 153, 193
abuse, 38, 39, 43, 49, 88,
   114, 126, 130, 131, 142,
   143, 157
acceptance, 11, 17, 22, 30,
   38, 41, 43, 48, 54, 69, 70,
   71, 72, 81, 94, 105, 108,
   109, 119, 121, 122, 153,
   162, 163, 164, 172
acupuncture, 94
addiction, 30, 34, 141, 142,
   143
adept, 98
adoption, 48, 109, 186
adrenal, 90

adult, 7, 10, 28, 29, 33, 38,
   47, 48, 49, 50, 52, 54, 55,
   57, 58, 59, 107, 108, 116,
   138, 160, 174
affinity, 92, 93
agreement, 25, 26, 30, 32,
   33, 35, 40, 43, 44, 47, 51,
   56, 60, 61, 62, 64, 70,
   106, 140
amusement, 35, 83
angels, 1, 18, 24, 31, 129,
   135, 136, 137, 138, 139,
   140, 143, 144
anger, 41, 78, 79, 120, 131,
   166, 169, 175
ankles, 94
appetite, 81
arms, 87, 179, 180, 187

astral, 66, 96, 97, 98, 99,
   100, 101, 102
astrological, 34
atmosphere, 139, 148
atoms, 6, 85
aura, 104, 181, 182, 183,
   187
awakening, 2, 3, 17, 55, 56,
   63, 82, 97, 99, 101, 140,
   147, 153, 154, 155, 161,
   162, 163, 190

babies, 24, 25, 26, 27, 30,
   33, 35, 36, 38, 45, 47, 132
bad, 10, 47, 48, 70, 72, 80,
   88, 126, 145
balance, 3, 4, 8, 10, 11, 12,
   13, 15, 20, 22, 40, 48, 87,
   156, 157, 174, 177, 179,
   190
baptism, 21
beauty, 1, 5, 17, 108, 114,
   147, 164, 191
Bible, 99, 146
birds, 7
birth, 19, 21, 23, 24, 26, 27,
   28, 29, 30, 31, 32, 33, 34,
   35, 36, 38, 40, 41, 42, 44,
   47, 52, 55, 57, 61, 64, 70,
   106, 115, 124, 153
blessing, 17, 21, 133, 193
blood, 87, 92, 93
bones, 28, 86, 87, 88, 94, 95
brain, 28, 85, 93, 160
breath, 65, 110, 148, 169,
   184
brothers, 47, 155
Buddha, 39, 56, 57, 58

cancer, 61, 89
celibacy, 10
cells, 90, 94, 113, 168, 190
centering, 164, 165, 192
ceremonies, 21
chakras, 8, 67, 76, 88, 90,
   91, 92, 93, 102, 115, 204
change, 8, 14, 15, 22, 41, 52,
   55, 56, 63, 69, 85, 94,
   105, 108, 110, 112, 123,
   131, 132, 138, 139, 140,
   151, 152, 153, 154, 156,
   157, 159, 160, 163, 172,
   174, 177, 179, 187, 188
channeling, 79
channels, 87, 129, 167, 178,
   179, 180, 187
children, 2, 3, 6, 7, 14, 15,
   16, 20, 23, 24, 25, 26, 28,
   30, 32, 33, 35, 38, 39, 41,
   43, 44, 45, 47, 48, 49, 50,
   51, 54, 55, 56, 58, 59, 60,
   80, 85, 87, 104, 107, 108,
   115, 120, 128, 130, 136,
   137, 138, 140, 144, 147,
   153, 160, 165, 174, 182
choices, 4, 5, 8, 12, 14, 20,
   21, 23, 28, 30, 34, 43, 51,
   59, 61, 74, 81, 91, 105,
   111, 137, 141, 144, 158,
   159, 160
Christian, 70, 99, 146
church, 45, 120, 158
circulation, 94
clairaudience, 119, 128, 129
clairvoyance, 33, 42, 93, 97
clergy, 51, 158
commitment, 39, 69, 77, 123

communication
  clear, 33, 67, 68, 80
  emotional, 127, 128
  non-verbal, 127
  spiritual, 24, 32, 35, 121,
    130, 140, 190, 193
communication with God,
  133, 158, 161, 165, 192
compassion, 43, 154
competition, 47, 57, 76, 84,
  87, 115, 136, 140, 141,
  158
complexity, 19, 65, 184, 191
conception, 19, 23, 24, 25,
  26, 27, 32, 36, 44, 46, 132
conflict, 32, 39, 42, 51, 74
confusion, 22, 25, 39, 48,
  50, 62, 74, 76, 79, 97,
  105, 110, 120, 131, 132,
  138, 157, 165
consciousness, 8, 10, 11, 13,
  17, 31, 35, 41, 44, 55, 56,
  57, 62, 74, 92, 97, 98,
  108, 109, 114, 117, 119,
  121, 126, 129, 131, 138,
  146, 170, 174, 175, 177,
  179, 188
control, 7, 10, 11, 13, 23, 35,
  54, 65, 66, 74, 77, 78, 79,
  80, 85, 90, 92, 93, 94,
  105, 111, 114, 115, 116,
  120, 121, 122, 127, 128,
  133, 168, 169, 170, 171,
  175, 177, 182
cords, 62, 168, 169, 174,
  178, 179, 180, 183, 187
Cosmic Consciousness, 113,
  133, 141

cosmic energy, 9, 16, 88,
  177, 178, 179, 180, 187
Cosmos, 9, 34, 40, 177
couples, 24, 26, 28, 35
creating and destroying, 165,
  175, 180
cycles, 9, 23, 30, 34, 39, 40,
  62, 63, 74, 174

death, 19, 23, 24, 43, 47, 57,
  60, 61, 62, 63, 64, 89,
  100, 101, 108, 137, 138,
  141, 142, 153
decisions, 10, 26, 34, 35, 41,
  46, 52, 55, 59, 61, 65, 68,
  71, 105, 106, 113, 121,
  123, 151, 161, 174, 187
deeds, 11, 118, 122, 123,
  124, 133
dependence, 27, 43, 45, 49,
  51, 66, 138
deprogramming, 69, 73,
  166, 186, 187, 188
desires, 26, 51, 52, 61, 68,
  74, 78, 79, 80, 81, 111,
  142, 152, 155, 164
destruction, 5, 8, 38, 44, 62,
  108, 112, 116, 124, 125,
  126, 147, 148, 151, 152,
  156, 157, 158, 165, 174,
  175, 177, 178, 180, 184,
  187, 188, 191, 193
devils, 135, 140, 141, 142,
  143, 144
dichotomies, 4, 10, 11, 12,
  13, 14, 22, 135, 177
digestion, 89
dimensions, 44, 102

discipline, 77, 87, 131, 166
divas, 18, 139
dolphins, 154
doubt, 22, 57, 81, 82, 84,
    136, 147, 161
dreams, 97, 126, 157
drugs, 30, 141, 143, 144,
    158, 190

ear, 166
earthbound, 143, 144
earthquake, 16, 85
Eden, 3, 146
effort, 57, 76, 98, 100, 115,
    136, 153, 166, 172
ego, 3, 142
Einstein, Albert, 83
emotions, 9, 16, 22, 27, 28,
    29, 38, 50, 61, 66, 67, 73,
    77, 78, 79, 80, 81, 88, 92,
    93, 94, 100, 114, 115,
    118, 119, 120, 127, 128,
    138, 141, 142, 164, 169,
    171, 174, 175, 176, 188,
    189, 191, 192
energy
    body, 65, 76, 128, 166
    cosmic, 9, 16, 177, 178,
        179, 180, 187
    creative, 88
    earth, 1, 4, 6, 7, 8, 9, 13,
        15, 18, 150, 177, 178,
        179, 180, 187, 188
    emotional, 38, 88, 127,
        169, 188
    female, 87
    foreign, 68, 69, 73, 88,
        89, 121
    God's, 156
    healing, 42
    kundalini, 87
    male, 87
    neutral, 188
    physical, 127, 164
    sexual, 79
    spiritual, 2, 6, 7, 26, 76,
        84, 87, 88, 94, 100,
        154, 157, 160
    survival, 76
    unwanted, 121, 174, 175,
        180, 182
energy body, 96, 99, 137
energy centers (see chakras),
    8, 67, 76, 168, 177, 178
energy channels, 88
energy lines, 7, 8
energy points, 94
enlightenment, 56, 68, 103
enthusiasm, 40, 42, 43, 57,
    64, 90
environment, 20, 21, 51, 67,
    81, 92, 114, 118, 120,
    121, 127, 151, 152, 153,
    155, 158, 171
ethics, 11, 25, 47, 52, 70, 71,
    72, 78, 80
evil, 12, 72, 160
evolution, 56, 76, 104, 108,
    109, 156
evolvement, 19, 85, 103
expectations, 25, 38, 56, 92,
    148, 167, 192

facades, 122
faith, 51, 82, 84, 161, 188

family, 20, 35, 41, 49, 52, 59, 61, 77, 101, 166, 170

fantasies, 10, 11, 104, 126, 127

fathers, 20, 24, 25, 28, 29, 34, 35, 36, 41, 42, 48, 49, 50, 61, 86, 100, 130, 137

fear, 5, 12, 26, 29, 32, 33, 41, 45, 49, 51, 59, 60, 62, 63, 64, 69, 72, 73, 78, 79, 82, 87, 88, 105, 120, 128, 130, 131, 132, 136, 141, 143, 144, 147, 148, 155, 160, 161, 166, 168, 186

feelings, 3, 12, 40, 50, 65, 74, 79, 108, 120, 143, 168, 182, 192

feet, 36, 46, 58, 94, 119, 137, 167, 172, 177, 181

female, 9, 35, 79, 87, 88, 91

fertility, 153

fetal, 27, 28, 29, 31, 106

fitness, 2

flexibility, 93, 159

focus, 6, 9, 16, 19, 21, 24, 31, 39, 42, 44, 50, 65, 67, 72, 74, 76, 82, 84, 87, 104, 105, 109, 110, 111, 112, 114, 116, 125, 127, 132, 142, 157, 158, 163, 164, 166, 171, 172, 177, 182, 184, 185, 188, 190

forgiveness, 185

formulas, 129

freedom, 5, 10, 11, 12, 17, 21, 22, 43, 45, 56, 57, 60, 61, 62, 76, 89, 98, 136, 139, 141, 142, 143, 144, 145, 166, 179, 181

friends, 2, 15, 24, 25, 27, 29, 32, 42, 43, 47, 55, 61, 78, 118, 121, 128, 129, 132, 133, 137, 140, 166, 167

funerals, 21

fury, 126, 128

Gabriel, 138

Gandhi, 58, 60

gender, 91

gestation, 27

ghosts, 101

glands, 90, 93, 172

God, 5, 12, 15, 18, 31, 40, 42, 43, 44, 55, 56, 57, 64, 70, 71, 73, 76, 83, 90, 95, 106, 113, 116, 120, 133, 134, 136, 139, 140, 141, 143, 144, 145, 153, 154, 156, 157, 158, 159, 161, 163, 165, 166, 167, 174, 181, 184, 185, 190, 191, 192, 193, 194

gonads, 91, 93

good, 2, 10, 12, 28, 47, 48, 70, 72, 80, 85, 125, 145, 146, 174

grace, 1, 160

grandparents, 20, 24, 66

gravity, 98, 115, 153

great teachers, 98, 99, 103, 133, 153

grief, 22, 153, 175

grounding, 77, 101, 166, 167, 168, 169, 170, 172, 174, 175, 179, 180

growth, 1, 4, 5, 9, 10, 11, 12,
16, 17, 19, 21, 22, 23, 27,
28, 32, 38, 47, 48, 50, 51,
54, 55, 56, 57, 58, 59, 60,
63, 68, 82, 85, 106, 107,
108, 115, 124, 125, 126,
139, 146, 153, 154, 157,
158, 160, 177, 183
guidance, 5, 21, 24, 71, 72,
105, 129, 160, 193
guides, 20, 21, 30, 33, 96,
101, 129, 138, 141, 142,
143
guilt, 181, 192

habits, 69
hands, 59, 94, 119, 138, 167,
172, 178, 180, 187
happiness, 25, 39, 77, 114,
117
harmony, 10, 11, 17, 26, 68,
75, 117, 153, 155, 164,
193
hate, 5, 12, 22, 42, 50, 54,
60, 69, 72, 73, 86, 88,
112, 122, 123, 124, 126,
141, 147, 148, 151, 157,
188
Hawaii, 1, 124, 125, 139
head, 24, 33, 47, 67, 85,
119, 165, 171, 172, 173,
174, 175, 177, 178, 179,
180, 181, 182, 184, 187,
191, 192, 193
healing, 3, 8, 10, 23, 27, 29,
31, 38, 39, 50, 55, 56, 84,
87, 89, 94, 101, 108, 122,
123, 143, 151, 152, 154,
156, 157, 177, 186
health, 2, 3, 8, 22, 29, 83,
86, 148, 150
heart, 92, 93, 110, 184
heaven, 5
hell, 5, 160
hierarchy, 137
hips, 119
humans, 1, 2, 5, 6, 8, 14, 16,
56, 65, 66, 70, 71, 77, 84,
119, 135, 137, 138, 139,
155, 160

illness, 22, 29, 42, 66, 88,
90, 95, 147
imagination, 7, 95, 126
imbalance, 66, 94, 154
immaturity, 50, 64, 84, 174
immortality, 101, 154
indigestion, 91
individuality, 5, 21, 34, 71,
76, 117, 135, 146, 157,
158, 159, 160
infants, 38
inner space, 103, 104, 109,
110, 111, 112, 113, 115,
116
inner voice, 67, 73, 128,
131, 132
insanity, 160
inspiration, 1, 55, 59, 83
instincts, 77
intellect, 33, 40, 65, 67, 71,
81, 82, 83, 84, 85, 93,
115, 132, 136, 138, 148,
190

intelligence, 27, 50, 151, 174
intestines, 88
intuition, 83

jealousy, 60
Jesus, 56, 57, 58, 70, 93, 99, 120, 144, 153
joy, 17, 18, 22, 25, 26, 36, 38, 41, 55, 90, 100, 114, 133, 140, 141, 150, 153, 154, 160, 162
judgement, 11, 20, 30, 69, 87, 141, 151, 158, 167, 172

karate, 166, 167
karma, 11, 13
King, Martin Luther, Jr. 59, 60
knowingness, 86
kundalini, 87

laughter, 100, 166, 167
legs, 94, 178, 179, 180, 187
levitation, 66
lies, 44, 46, 56, 138
life path, 21, 44, 52
limits, 14, 16, 27, 34, 56, 57, 58, 60, 66, 67, 72, 81, 82, 83, 84, 85, 97, 100, 120, 136, 137, 148, 153, 154, 171, 192
logic, 97, 104
loneliness, 43
lotus, 174
love, 3, 5, 12, 22, 24, 26, 35, 38, 39, 43, 54, 55, 56, 57,
58, 60, 64, 67, 68, 70, 71, 73, 74, 89, 94, 100, 110, 118, 120, 123, 130, 141, 142, 144, 150, 153, 155, 157, 158, 161, 164, 165, 188, 194

male, 9, 35, 79, 87, 88, 91, 130
man, 10, 12, 13, 24, 33, 42, 49, 51, 58, 99, 113, 114, 115, 126
marriage, 24, 26, 39, 55, 68, 73, 110, 174
masculine, 39, 49
mates, 76
maturity, 4, 5, 9, 14, 16, 50, 61, 64, 84, 106, 159, 174
meditation, 23, 26, 27, 28, 29, 32, 38, 40, 42, 44, 54, 55, 56, 58, 60, 68, 69, 73, 79, 86, 90, 93, 94, 101, 115, 121, 123, 127, 131, 140, 143, 161, 165, 166, 167, 172, 176, 177, 179, 180, 185, 187, 190, 191, 192, 193
memory, 71, 97, 115
mental image pictures, 28, 29, 97, 128, 129, 130, 131, 165, 175, 186, 188
messengers, 159
Michael, 138
ministers, 80
miracles, 84, 137, 153
missionaries, 151
mother, 20, 24, 25, 27, 28, 29, 30, 31, 32, 33, 34, 35,

36, 41, 42, 43, 45, 46, 47,
48, 49, 50, 51, 87, 89,
106, 182
mountains, 2, 148
muscles, 93

nature spirits, 139
negative, 80
neutrality, 11, 43, 51, 78,
120, 121, 128, 138, 154,
164, 171, 172, 188
New Testament, 99
night, 1, 69, 99, 100, 125,
148, 166
Nightingale, Florence, 59,
60

opposites, 4, 10, 12, 30, 73,
80, 122, 135
organs, 28, 90, 94, 95

paradise, 147, 148, 149, 194
parents, 20, 24, 25, 26, 28,
35, 45, 47, 49, 51, 66,
105, 106, 110, 130, 142,
182, 186
past lives, 38, 39, 55, 56,
186
Pele, 1, 139
perseverance, 59
pets, 128
pineal, 93, 172
pituitary, 93
poles, 80
pollution, 148
positive, 80
power, 1, 5, 6, 7, 8, 16, 18,
26, 35, 46, 48, 52, 57, 67,

79, 80, 85, 87, 92, 101,
102, 110, 113, 115, 119,
120, 121, 122, 123, 124,
126, 127, 132, 141, 143,
158, 164, 185, 188
prayer, 108, 133, 150
pregnancy, 23, 28, 29, 30,
31, 42, 43, 132
prejudice, 11, 59, 72
present time, 23, 110, 184
privacy, 125
programming, 20, 66, 69,
70, 72, 73, 101, 115, 186
promiscuity, 126
puberty, 52, 54, 160
pyramids, 8

realignment, 158
recycling, 150
reflexology, 94
reincarnation, 9, 13, 113
relationships, 2, 5, 20, 34,
39, 40, 41, 42, 44, 48, 53,
55, 56, 67, 70, 76, 83, 89,
92, 94, 100, 114, 116,
121, 148, 152, 159, 164,
165, 166, 169, 185, 190
religion, 115, 151, 186
reprogramming, 186, 188
resistance, 11, 143
responsibilities, 11, 13, 14,
21, 41, 44, 46, 50, 51, 71,
72, 80, 95, 106, 109, 111,
140, 142, 146, 148, 150,
151, 161, 175, 182, 190
rites of passage, 19, 21, 22,
49, 61
ritual, 61

roses, 175, 182, 184, 187, 188, 191, 193
rules, 13, 59, 70, 71, 72, 73, 74, 80

sadness, 114, 117
sanity, 161
seniority, 20, 57, 58, 62, 65, 66, 72, 76, 77, 81, 83, 114, 151, 162
senses, 3, 31, 44, 46, 47, 54, 65, 81, 97, 104, 148
sensuality, 20, 153
sexuality, 10, 13, 49, 52, 66, 67, 74, 78, 79, 80, 81, 85, 114, 115, 126, 141, 143, 158, 171, 190
shame, 181
siblings, 20, 34, 45, 66
silver cord, 62
sin, 80
Skelton, Red, 12, 13
sleep, 45, 83, 98, 99, 133, 147, 172
smell, 28, 65
spine, 76, 87, 88, 167, 168, 178, 180
spirit and body, 48, 67, 68, 72, 76, 131, 164
spirit guides, 24, 72, 129, 160
spirits, 136, 139
spiritual agreements, 25, 26, 44
spiritual body, 28
spiritual communication, 24, 32, 35, 121, 130, 140, 190, 193

spiritual control, 11, 13, 54, 85, 170, 175
spiritual creativity, 6, 9, 55, 56, 58, 67, 76, 82, 85, 86, 88, 90, 91, 93, 99, 102, 116, 118, 162
spiritual cycles, 23
spiritual development, 19, 21, 46, 48, 55, 56, 115
spiritual enlightenment, evolvement, 56, 85, 103
spiritual frontier, 1, 4
spiritual information, 7, 62, 68, 84, 85, 94, 115, 150, 151
spiritual lessons, 10
spiritual maturity, 4, 9, 14, 106
spiritual nature, 2, 6, 15, 16, 17, 19, 36, 55, 147, 190
spiritual path, 59, 141, 144
spiritual perspective, 23, 24, 25, 28, 40, 62, 63, 69, 84, 88, 139, 147, 148, 152, 159, 160, 161, 165, 180
spiritual purpose, 3, 40, 54, 55, 59, 78, 104, 116, 144
spiritual reality, 12, 17, 63, 125
spiritual sight (see clairvoyance), 6, 86, 171
spiritual source, 48
spiritual stages, 22, 54, 62
spiritual teachings, 115
spiritual techniques, 73, 163, 164, 165, 166, 187, 204
spiritual textbooks, 166

spiritual vibration, 16, 106, 108
spiritualize, 60, 87
spiritualizing the body, 87
stomach, 89, 91
strength, 14, 20, 39, 43, 48, 50, 52, 55, 59, 70, 79, 81, 93, 109, 122, 123, 141, 148, 152, 157, 158
stress, 157
suffering, 22, 56, 61
sun, 2, 9
survival, 20, 29, 51, 66, 72, 76, 77, 81, 91, 93, 140, 159, 171
symbols, 56, 67, 94, 128, 129, 153, 174, 175, 186
sympathy, 138

telekinesis, 66
telepathy, 85, 119, 128, 129
temptation, 143, 144
Ten Commandments, 70
therapy, 163, 190
thoughts, 2, 3, 10, 11, 14, 23, 40, 81, 104, 109, 118, 124, 125, 126, 127, 128, 130, 133, 140, 148, 153, 164, 184
throat, 67

thyroid, 93
time and space, 9, 13, 14, 15, 16, 57, 66, 98, 115, 171, 184, 187
timelessness, 15
transformation, 61, 140

unique personality, 49
unlearning, 182

victims, 106
visions, 157
volcanoes, 1, 16, 18, 139, 174

war, 32, 99, 148
water, 98, 148, 153
weakness, 14, 50, 52, 81, 109, 123
weather, 16, 174
weddings, 21, 153
whales, 17, 154
will, 20
wisdom, 2, 3, 40, 154
womb, 27, 29, 30, 70, 87
women, 10, 25, 30, 31, 39, 49, 51, 55, 59, 80, 114, 130, 142

yoga, 104

ABOUT THE AUTHOR

Mary Ellen Flora was born in Virginia in 1944. She received a BA in Sociology from Queens College in Charlotte, NC and did graduate work in Education and Counseling at Oregon State University in Corvallis, OR. She has taught pre-kindergarten, junior high and high school and was a Youth Program Director for the YMCA.

In 1976, she and her husband, M.F. "Doc" Slusher, founded the Church of Divine Man/CDM Psychic Institute in the Pacific Northwest. Mary Ellen is currently a Bishop with the Church. Through her work, she has helped thousands of people get in touch with their psychic abilities and their spiritual awareness.

Mary Ellen is listed in the twenty-fifth edition of *Who's Who in the West.*

ABOUT CDM PUBLICATIONS

CDM Publications is a small press offering books and tapes of a spiritual nature. If you have questions or comments or are interested in learning more about meditation, healing, clairvoyance or other topics concerning spiritual awareness, please contact us.

CDM Publications
2402 Summit Ave.
Everett, WA 98201
(206) 259-9322

CDM PUBLICATIONS 2402 Summit Ave. ▪ Everett, WA 98201

Phone (206) 259-9322 ▪ Fax (206) 259-5109 ▪ Toll Free 1-800-360-6509

		QUANTITY	TOTAL
THE ENERGY SERIES BOOKS by Mary Ellen Flora			
Cosmic Energy: *The Creative Power*	$12.00	_____	_____
Earth Energy: *The Spiritual Frontier*	$12.00	_____	_____
THE KEY SERIES BOOKS by Mary Ellen Flora			
Meditation: *Key to Spiritual Awakening*	$7.95	_____	_____
Healing: *Key to Spiritual Balance*	$7.95	_____	_____
Clairvoyance: *Key to Spiritual Perspective*	$10.00	_____	_____
Chakras: *Key to Spiritual Opening*	$10.00	_____	_____
THE KEY SERIES AUDIO CASSETTES by Mary Ellen Flora			
Meditation: *Key to Spiritual Awakening*	$9.95	_____	_____
Healing: *Key to Spiritual Balance*	$9.95	_____	_____
Clairvoyance: *Key to Spiritual Perspective*	$10.00	_____	_____
Chakras: *Key to Spiritual Opening*	$10.00	_____	_____
OTHER PUBLICATIONS AVAILABLE			
I Believe: *Sermons* by M. F. "Doc" Slusher	$15.00	_____	_____
CDM Hymnal	$15.00	_____	_____

Sub-Total _____

Shipping & Handling _____

Tax (7.9% WA residents only) _____

Total _____

SHIPPING & HANDLING: $2.00 first item, 75¢ each additional item

---

Prices and availability subject to change without notice.
Please allow 6 weeks for delivery. No cash or COD.

☐ VISA ☐ MasterCard ☐ Call me for credit info - Phone _____

Card #_____Exp. Date_____

Signature_____

Name_____

Address_____

City/State_____Zip_____